"This book tells how I'm trying to stop listening to the voice of the phony self and trying to tune in to the voice of the true self which is the higher self. The more I learn to do that, the more I get in harmony with myself, the people I love and society in general. The result is a spiritual psychology that gives a different way of looking at and working on the common problems of life. It's helped me see that instead of being a worm, that I was a wonder . . . and that you are a wonder, too."

—Jess Lair

Fawcett Crest Books
by Jess Lair, Ph.D.:

"AIN'T I A WONDER . . . AND AIN'T YOU
A WONDER TOO!"

"HEY GOD, WHAT SHOULD I DO
NOW?"

"I AIN'T MUCH, BABY—BUT I'M
ALL I'VE GOT"

"I AIN'T WELL—BUT I SURE
AM BETTER"

SEX: IF I DIDN'T LAUGH I'D CRY

"AIN'T I A WONDER ... AND AIN'T YOU A WONDER, TOO!"

Winning Freedom Through Acceptance

Jess Lair, Ph.D.

FAWCETT CREST • NEW YORK

Dedication

This book is dedicated to all those people who have come into my heart and loved me so warmly and so well. This is my progress report on how I am doing as I proceed on my spiritual quest. And it is my progress report to all the people who have read my previous books, told me their stories, wished me well, or just quietly went about doing what they saw was important for them in the new light that we shed on each other's true path.

Contents

"AIN'T I A WONDER ... AND AIN'T YOU A WONDER, TOO!"

Winning Freedom Through Acceptance

ONE

I Had My Head Buried in My Navel

I want to share with you some things it has taken me a long time to learn. Yet now I see these ideas were always there waiting for me to find them. Maybe you've started to make some of these discoveries yourself.

I've spent a lot of time trying to figure out why I've had so much trouble in life. Often I seem to be one of the lowest common denominators. I seem to make all the mistakes. And I seem to make a lot of them in much greater style than most people, so my mistakes are painfully obvious to me and the people around me. I don't know why this is the course that has, in a sense, been laid out for me, but my job seems to be to pound my head against a cement wall over and over and over again until finally I'm bloody and battered enough that I finally realize, "Hey, I think I should stop doing this."

I remind myself of an old teacher of mine, an alcoholic

11

who went way down to the bottom in skid row. He was about as beat up by life as you could possibly be.

After he had come back from the depths, he was able to tell us so many wonderful things he had learned so he could get his life straightened out. Someone said to him, "Vince, I think you were sent down there to skid row so you could come back and tell all the rest of us what it was like so we wouldn't have to go down that far."

I haven't traveled the skid rows of the big cities. But I have spent an awful lot of time on the skid rows of the mind.

I've lived with my head so deeply buried in my own navel that most of life passed me by unnoticed. I've spent my life, like the Type A's Meyer Friedman describes in *Type A Behavior and Your Heart*, rushing through life.

I didn't know where I was going but I was sure going to get there fast. I hurried so much I missed everything. And still I'm hard-core Type A and I'm sure I'm going to stay Type A all the rest of my life. Any progress I make, I sure make awfully slow. I don't give up easily on anything. And moderation just ain't my dish.

I think probably the best characterization you could make of me at this point is I'm a man in search of my being. I'm trying to get a clearer sense of what I was meant to be and be it.

I spent the first thirty-five years of my life running from that being. I spent the first thirty-five years of my life without any respect for what I was. I spent the first thirty-five years of my life working off policy statements as to what I wanted to do so that I could satisfy this monstrous ego of mine. My goals were to impress other people, put other people down, intimidate them, and put them in a subsidiary position. Never in those times did I give any thought to what I was and what I was truly meant to be. I was using myself in the same way that you buy a tool and use it. But I was like a person who would buy a light and delicate tool and use it for a monkey wrench or a hammer. I had no respect for what I was.

When I had my heart attack at thirty-five, that was the first experience that drastically showed me that I was heading the wrong way in life. All of a sudden, I had this deep, deep awakening like some inner part of me was finally allowed a chance to express itself and talk. And that deep inner voice was able to say, "Hey, you're a long way from anything you believe in. You're not doing the things that are right for you. You've made a whole bunch of destructive choices and they have taken you way off into an area in which you don't belong. Right then, I decided: Never again would I do anything I didn't believe in.

That was fifteen years ago. Since that time my search for what I believed in, my search for my being, has been uppermost in my mind. Since then, the confusion in my sick mind has been slowly clearing up, my body has been slowly healing and restoring itself, and a lot of wonderful things have come about for me because of that process.

Rencently I spent three days in British Columbia helicopter skiing in the powder snow at 10,000 feet with my three sons, my son-in-law, and a friend. The six of us had a beautiful time. The helicopter would drop us in the high mountain country and we would ski down. For the first four runs each day I could keep up with the boys and the fifth run they would have to make on their own. But I was really thrilled to be able to do such a thing at my advanced and decrepit age. It was a beautiful example for me of the marvelous recuperative powers of the human body once we start getting things a little straightened out in our minds.

I started to learn after my first heart attack. But the

damage that I had done to my body was still there and I was bothered by constant pain in my heart, which was a threat and a frightening thing because every time I would have a pain in my chest, I would wonder, "Hey, is this the sign I'm going under?" I found it was very, very difficult living life under that kind of threat.

I had heart surgery and that helped remove the angina. But the week I had heart surgery, there were five of us operated on and only two lived. It was another reminder I was not going to live forever and I'd better not endlessly postpone living until some future day. So I continued to learn. It was easier because my angina, the constant reminder of death, was taken away. I think we need to know and accept our death. But I don't think it can be too constant a thing. I think we need to know and accept death and then put it aside.

I continued to make mistakes and I continued to learn. It seemed like I would learn something and then take the very thing I had learned and twist and distort it so much I would turn it into an instrument of my death.

I think partly because of some new mistakes, I developed a tumor in my stomach and was flown back to the hospital in Minneapolis. The doctors opened me up, saw I had an inoperable tumor, and sewed me back up. They said, "You've got stomach cancer and you'll be dead in three weeks. You'll never make it back to Montana." It turned out they were wrong but they sure got my attention for a moment.

I have been forced to look at some things in a way that very few people have. Furthermore, it seems self-analysis is something I have a special aptitude for. I have spent so much time in those fifteen years since my heart attack talking to people, one at a time, ten at a time, two thousand at a time, about the ideas that are in my books, the ideas I have been seeking to help me live better. And there is almost no situation in which I feel more natural or which I feel is more right for me than talking about some of the discoveries I have made about learning to live. So perhaps one crucial part of this being that I have been in search for is that I am a teacher.

In *Little Big Man,* there is a line where Little Big Man is saved from the Custer battlefield. He is the only white man that comes off that battlefield alive. He wakes up in Old Lodge Skin's teepee and realizes that he isn't dead. And he says, "When you should have died and didn't you ain't never the same." That is kind of what happened to me. Largely I find it is a good thing to be aware of the sweetness of life, but I notice occasionally it is a bit of an obsession. I have such an impatience with people in some ways. Some student will stop by and say, "Jess, I was just killing a little time so I thought I would stop by and talk to you." I want to jump off my chair, grab him by the throat, and choke him to death for talking about killing time, for taking time so lightly. Or, I will walk out of our office building with some of our faculty and it's snowing outside. In Bozeman it snows seven or eight months of the year even though it is warm enough that the snow soon melts. Someone will say, "Oh, what a terrible day." Again I want to yell at him because when you should have died and didn't there aren't any terrible days. They are all beautiful. So I get carried away on that a little bit.

In the early days I wondered why life was so screwed up. I wondered why the world was so terrible. As I look back now I see it in a different perspective. I ran into a story in Bozeman that dramatized some of the problems I see in my life.

We have some of the finest trout streams in the nation near us in the Gallatin Valley. We have blue-ribbon trout streams like the Madison, the Gallatin, and the Yellowstone, streams that are legendary in the world of trout fishing. To increase the trout, they were raising trout in hatcheries and stocking them in the streams. But it didn't seem to improve the fishing as much as they hoped it would. So one very clever scientist did an experiment. He blocked off a mile of the Madison and allowed no fishing. There were about 2,000 fish per mile before he planted 500 fish. He came back about two months later to see how many fish were left. He found to his horror that there weren't 2,500 fish. There weren't even 2,000 fish. There were about 1,800 fish left.

What had happened? Well, what had happened is that when you put into the Madison six-inch hatchery trout that had been raised in concrete runways, those trout had no sense of the natural territory that trout acquire when they are raised in the wild. And those hatchery trout, in their frantic dashing around in the stream to secure food for themselves and in their lack of understanding of territories, had so traumatized the native trout that they killed off some of them as well as themselves.

If you would have asked this hatchery trout, then, to describe the world of trout, he would have described it as a place in which all the trout he saw were frantically running from him. And I saw that was just the way I would have described my life before my heart attack and for some time after. Whenever I would come on the scene, people couldn't get away from me fast enough. It wasn't just paranoid of me to think that I would come into a gathering and start talking and pretty soon everyone would run and go in the opposite direction. Then I would say, "What a terrible world this is." But now I have seen there is a different view of it, I have come to see that I was causing most of the behavior toward me that I found so troubling.

Like the hatchery trout, I was coming at others hard and tough. I had no feeling for people and no kindness, and no compassion and no understanding for them. But I would then turn around and be alarmed because these people were running away from me.

Now if you would take that hatchery trout and lift him a mile upstream, he would see a world where the natural trout are sitting in their own environmental niches happy in their little pools and in their quiet waters behind the rocks. There is a bit of jostling for territory but it is not a very serious thing. And he would say, "My God, this can't be the world of trout because this isn't the frantic running away from each other that I know." And then of course, you'd have to tell the hatchery trout, "That's true. But that very thing you describe is what you cause. Most often you are the problem."

I am in the same position. I have lived in a world where I was the problem. I desperately needed and wanted to believe that you folks are the problem and I am not. What I hated to believe but what I have been forced to believe is that I am the problem and you folks are not. I have been given a glimpse of a beautiful world where I can live in harmony and not be much of a problem. I've seen enough now to know that for many folks that isn't a terrifying, horrifying world out there. My students used to say to me, "Jess, this is terrible, what you're doing. You're giving us this vision of a beautiful, wonderful life. We're experiencing, in this classroom, some love and acceptance and a feeling that we've always hungered for. In a way, you're doing a cruel thing to us by holding up this beautiful vision of life. But we're going to have to walk out this door and face that world outside."

I knew of the tremendous cruelties outside that door. I knew of the anger, I knew of the discrimination, I knew of the injustices, I knew of all the hurts. So I didn't have a very good answer for their questions. I would say, "Well, at least you can be forewarned so you're braced for some of the things that are going to happen. That way things can be a little better for you."

What I've come to see now is a different view of that world out there. Believe me, I can't get it into focus very often, but I have been able to see that the world isn't horrifying or terrifying. Only my twisted perceptions of it and the way I come at it can make it so. Most of what I see out there, I'm creating. And the things I'm not creating, I'm distorting in my own mind.

What I want to talk to you about is a different way of looking at ourselves, at others, and at the world around us. I want to show you what my evidence is. These ideas are very precious to me. I have paid for them literally with my life's blood. I simply offer them to you so you can try them out and see if they work. I would be surprised if you didn't doubt or weren't troubled by much that I say because in the content and fabric within which you and I spend our lives, these ideas do not make sense. They run contrary to most of our deepest convictions. They are a challenge and an affront to the idea we hold most dear, and that is that I am not the problem.

All I ask of you, and I am a scientist, is that you give this set of ideas as careful a hearing as you can. Draw from them a set of things that you can try, little experiments. Then go and try them out for yourself. I have found that for me they do work when I can manage the courage, when I can get the strength to give any one of them even a halfhearted try.

Before I had my heart attack in February 1962, if you

would have asked me what my dream was, I could not have conceived for myself something like what I have now. And this is one advantage that I have, and one of the things that makes me a pretty good teacher. I've done, as near as I can see, everything wrong. I have learned everything the hardest, hardest way. I am not like a gifted athlete skier. You ask him how he skis and I think he is hard-pressed to tell you because he just came on to it smoothly and easily and naturally. He often doesn't make a very good teacher.

But a knuckle-headed, two-left-footed skier like me, who had to take thirty years to learn how to ski, can teach you because there isn't a mistake in skiing that I haven't made persistently and continuously.

I have been where the living was bad, as bad as anything can be. I have lived in the skid row of the mind. And to me that's worse than the skid row of the body, bad as that is. You can escape the physical skid row much easier than you can escape the skid row of the mind.

So fifteen years ago, if you had asked me, "Jess, what is your dream and describe it," I couldn't have conceived of anything as beautiful as what I'm experiencing just by my very limited abilities.

If, then, you had outlined for me the experiences in my life of the past week, as a typical week, I would have said, "Hey, that's impossible. And furthermore, if it is possible for me to have such a dream as that, it's too much. I don't want to ask for that much." It would have been like imagining you got all the presents at Christmas time, with nothing for anyone else. And that's greedy, that's taking too much. But yet what I've seen is that isn't the way this system works. The more you have, the more somebody else can have. We're working here with a different kind of system than that of the material plane where the more you have the less somebody else has. No, I couldn't have conceived a life like this despite all the problems I'm developing still, despite all my unwillingness and inability to do what I know I should do and could do.

I went from a person who was completely lost in self to a person who can see there is a power greater than myself. I went from a person who was completely self-centered to a person who is able to get out of self and get in harmony with a power other than myself. In other words, I went from a person who had his head buried in his own navel to a person who can get it out some of the time. I went from a person who was dominated by fear, anger, self-pity, and resentment to where I'm not so often in fear and anxiety, and to where I now spend some of my time with a measure of peace. I went from a person who didn't like what he was doing and felt trapped to where I have a life and work I love and where I have all the freedom I want already. I went from a person who was fighting all limitations and failing to know and accept those limitations to where I can practice quite a bit of acceptance and succeed at most everything I've attempted. I used to say the world was a terrifying, horrifying world. I now find it is a beautiful place that yields up each day lovely things for me that exceed my fondest expectations.

I can't recite all these good things without being honest. I can't leave out the other side of my life today. I can still sometimes feel saddened and overwhelmed to see how often I am such a very limited husband to my wife, a very limited father to my children, a very limited friend to my friends, and a very limited member of my various communities. But I am very happy and grateful for the progress I have made in being freed from some of the hold my compulsions had on me.

Most people don't understand their own compulsions. They are good at seeing the compulsions other people have but they are poor at seeing their own. I believe compulsions came out of obsessions. I believe obsessions are the roots underground. Compulsions are the tree you see above the ground. One of my basic obsessions is my desire to impress other people, to make them think well of me and put them below me so I can be on top. That obsession probably comes from my childish sense of inadequacy. I felt in my early childhood that I wasn't as good as other people so I think I became obsessed with a need to show people I was something. This, I think, led to my compulsion of bitter competitiveness in the classroom and in business. And it led to a use of houses, cars, clothes, and other symbols to impress people and put them down.

When I put my compulsions out in the open like that, it's easy to see why I needed to lie to myself so much. There is no way I could honestly justify my overdriven strivings. I had to lie to myself so I could continue to live with my compulsions. And just like the alcoholic, the worse my compulsions got, the more I lied to myself and denied the compulsions and the hold they had on me.

I was just like the alcoholic who claims he can take it or leave it completely alone. By his statement he tells you that he can't use alcohol moderately as other people do. He either takes it to drunkenness or has to leave it completely alone. Yet he thinks he is telling us how free he is to take it or leave it alone.

Neither he nor I were free. We were like puling slaves of our compulsions. All you had to do was offer me something that would make me look big and the people around me small and I would be your slave so I could have it. But the material things never worked, so I had to throw them away and try again. I couldn't break the compulsion, so I had to lie to myself and tell myself what I was doing was good, or at least, that everyone else was doing the same thing, so I wasn't wrong.

If you asked me if I was honest, I'd say sure I was honest. I didn't steal, so I was honest. I had "cash register" honesty, but that's honesty only by the narrowest and most legalistic interpretations of what honesty means. How can you call it honesty when you're lying to the most crucial person there is in the world, which is yourself?

I was lying to my wife, too. I thought I was a father. One night about 9 P.M. I came home after the kids were in bed and Jackie and I were watching television. There was a commercial on about some guy who was a big brother to some poor little underprivileged kid out of the ghetto. I said, "Boy, I should do that. I should be a big brother to some poor little kid, be a father to him." My wife said, "Why don't you try being a father to your own children first?" So that's lying to yourself. That's me lying to myself.

This isn't the kind of talk that lets you smile very much. I'm dealing off a cold deck and it isn't a pretty spectacle. I'm face to face with the only really horrifying part of that world out there, and that's the part I have had in creating that world for myself. And the part I've had in hanging on to and perpetuating unpleasant parts of that world.

What I see now is that world out there is like a gigantic big cafeteria. And all of us are helping ourselves to just exactly the things we need or want at the moment. And that's a horrible thought. "You mean to tell me, you no-good so and so, that I need and want all the various things that are such agony for me during the day?" And the answer is, "Yes, that's exactly what I presume to say."

Now we need to soften that up a bit. I was talking to a group of alcoholics about this cafeteria idea and some alcoholic's wife said afterwards, "Jess, I did not want an alcoholic husband." And the way she put her story, I told her, "Yes, I can see what you mean. You did not want an alcoholic husband and I'll go along with that." But the sadness is that she needed to have a husband she could look down on, an emotional cripple. And one kind of people we can look down on are those who have a weakness for the bottle and they go into alcoholism. When the husband went into alcoholism five, ten, or fifteen years later, the wife was faced with the kind of consequence she couldn't have anticipated earlier as the result of a previous decision. But she had bought some part of the package. In my experience, we all do. So it is with so many of the things I wanted in life. There were always encumbrances that came along with what I wanted. When I got that bad part of the deal there sure was a part of me that balked. But you can't have part of the deal and not all of it. You can't have a lot of Christmas presents without bills. There's just no way.

So that life out there, in my experience, is like a gigantic cafeteria. And each of us have the opportunity to pick and choose just exactly what we want.

I was reading a newspaper story about the black people who started the boycott of the buses in Montgomery, Alabama, twenty years ago, a crusade which was probably one of the most beautiful examples of co-operation among people that exists. Hundreds of black-owned vehicles were formed into a volunteer transportation company to bring black people to work and to school.

But some of the folks at Montgomery who had been leaders in the bus boycott were hurt because now they weren't getting the publicity they felt they deserved for their participation in the crusade.

Other people who participated equally, as near as I could see, had a good feeling about it. They felt, "Hey, I don't care that I don't get publicity, I don't care that I don't get recognized and other people are getting the recognition. What counts to me is that I was part of one huge motor pool functioning so my people knew they could always count on rides to work or school. We had this beautiful co-operation, yet adequate controls so all the chiselers were weeded out." There was no bad feeling and it was all a good feeling.

That's the kind of thing I'm speaking of. In one person's heart is bitterness and frustration and anger that he or she is not getting publicity and recognition. In another case, a person is getting the satisfaction that was truly there to be gotten, which is the feeling of participating in that particular job, one of the most crucial events in the black struggle for freedom. Two people went through the cafeteria of life and in a sense they got the same tray twenty years ago. They were both in the same experience. But they came out of it with two very different reactions.

This is the kind of thing I've seen over and over and that is so telling to me. I see a whole bunch of us getting exactly the same things and I see how I can screw them up. I have seen myself screw up a free lunch. No matter what gift you could give me, I could find something wrong with the gift or the way it was given. And the biggest, biggest problem of all is that I saw myself, like the meanest child in the world after opening all my presents, saying, "Is that all I got? How come somebody else has more presents than me? How come somebody else has bigger presents than me?" And I saw I was so insane the

24

only way to temporarily ease my insanity would have been for me to have all the presents. But then, after a minute or two, I would feel bad because the other people didn't have any. There's absolutely no way that unbalanced mind of mine could have had any degree or kind of satisfaction.

Much of this book is what was said to a group of psychiatric nurses in Columbus, Ohio, at a two-day seminar I presented to them in December 1975. I told my psychiatric nurses, "I know you're regularly dealing with people that society tends to call somewhat different. That is interesting, but to me the real insane people of this world aren't locked up. To me the real insane ones are the ones like me running around loose."

My insanity was so socially acceptable that it wasn't even noticeable and that's a travesty. I was felt by most of the people around me to be in good shape. If I would have died with the heart attack that I had in 1962, they would have said, "Hey, we're losing some of our best people so young. How come?"

Now isn't that sad? I was so far out. I was as nutty as any person psychiatric nurses deal with and yet the people would have written an obituary about the loss of this fine citizen. People who knew me would have talked about "Ain't it too bad?" That's a sign they didn't really know me. If they had, they would have said, "Thank God, we got rid of a bad apple, a person who was a source of grief and pain and infection to everybody around him."

I read a workingman's obituary in the Butte, Montana, newspaper. Butte's a nearby mining town where all the ethnics met and mingled years ago. Most obituaries talk about how you were a member of the Odd Fellows and all these other big deals and committees and organizations and stuff. But all they said about this fellow was "He was an ardent hunter and fisherman." I was surprised at first and then I thought, "Isn't that neat?" He's possibly a much saner man than most because he didn't need all these clubs, all these funny things like Cadillacs or a Ph.D., to be ego patches on a puny little personality.

He was an ardent hunter and a fisherman. I hope he didn't carry it to excess. I managed to. On opening day of hunting there was only one place that any self-respecting man should be and that was out there in the field hunting. If my wife would have died two days before the season opening, I would have said, "Freeze the body. We'll have a late funeral." Or I would have said, "Let's not make a fuss. She wouldn't have wanted that. So let's slip her in the ground real quick. I've got to go hunting tomorrow."

I managed to screw up a couple of beautiful avocations: hunting and fishing. Now, at least in my fishing, I do go when it's smooth and groovy to go. And when there's something important happening I stay home. In that small area of my life, some of the insanity is lifting, so there is hope for me. And, you could perhaps say, "Well, I'm sure glad to hear that good news. It's about time."

In the great cafeteria of life, there are various life styles. Many people defend their choice of life styles as being just right for them, but they are blind to the price tags on those life styles. "Hey, Jess, I've got this groovy life style. I've found you can't trust nobody. And you've got to be aggressive, man. You've got to shove and you've got to plan ahead and you've got to plan your work and work your plan. And when it comes to selling, man, you've got to use the hard way. And you've got to put the pressure in there because them good guys, they finish last. And you've got to get your business right now. Do that business today."

That's a nice, aggressive, coronary, Jess Lair–type life style. What's the price tag on that life style in the great cafeteria of life? Simple. Early, Type-A heart attack. A 75 per cent chance of living through the early heart attack. Chances are seven out of ten that there will be more heart attacks in the next ten years and increasing chances that one of those heart attacks will put you under.

That's just part of the price tag. There are some more things on the price tag and these are the really bad parts. What can be worse than dying? Simple. The living death. The living death is where you are so withdrawn from life that when you come to the end of each day you wonder, "Why did I bother living today?"

So it isn't so bad that you don't live so long. What's even worse is the way you live while you're around. And to me, what I've come to see now is that living death is the most chilling of all parts of the price tag on the heart attack life style or the life styles that go with any of the other compulsions.

Let's look at some of the other price tags. We're getting a pretty good idea what some of these price tags are now as we see that the mind and body are hooked together, not separate like we used to think they were.

"I've got this nice withdrawn personality and I don't want to say nothing but social conversation to nobody. I'll get up in the morning and I'll do my work and I'll come home and I'll read my paper and I'll watch my sports show and I'll go to bed. And I won't say much to anybody. I don't have feelings and the world is a pretty lousy place and who can expect anything out of a person who didn't have any more education and any more advantages than I did. I had to stay at home while my other brother went to college and he became a rich doctor. Just because my mother died, I had to do all these things." Self-pity, resentment, and hopelessness. One of the most common ways a self-pitying and resentful person dies is with cancer. And if he gets cancer, he's very likely to die about twice as fast as someone without those personality characteristics. And when he goes to radiology, and the radiologist happens to be the one in ten thousand who offers him his group therapy in addition to radiology as a treatment, he will probably be in the half of the cancer patients who refuse the therapy that could lengthen their lives.

It's a very simple therapy that's offered. What it basically consists of is visualizing three times a day that you and your body's immunological defenses are big and powerful like the huge gorillas that played pro football like Jerry Kramer and Fuzzy Thurston, that the cancer cells are little, puny things. And the big gorillas are going around stamping out these cancer cells with fists like picnic hams. And you visualize that process three times a day for about five minutes. And then you talk about it in the therapy sessions. Half of the people who are offered this therapy refuse it so they can speed up the process of their dying. Why? That's because the second part of the price tag says that when you aren't getting anything out of life deep down, why should you be interested in prolonging it? That's the chilling part of that price tag, that life gets so bad you won't take advantage of a chance to save yourself.

There's another personality style. I can describe it very accurately because I don't have good words for it, but I think you'll get the point. This is a person who, everything that happens, they turn inward. They worry constantly. Why are people looking at me? Are those people talking about me? What am I doing wrong? Everything goes inwaard and it eats up their stomach; they get

28

ulcers and then they bleed to death and die. Or, they have three fourths of their stomach taken out and live.

We also have our addictive and compulsive personalities. Some of us manage to catch two or three of these things at one time, like in my case. This is the kind of personality that turns to drugs and alcohol. The emotional pain of their loneliness is too much for them. They need something to numb the pain, they need their activities of one kind of another. My compulsive activities were by and large socially respectable, such as work, hobbies, and an undue involvement in clubs. I had a toastmasters group that I went to every Monday night and then played poker afterward trying to take money away from my friends. Beautiful. Unbelievably beautiful. You can imagine how they loved me. I was a pretty picture, I'll tell you.

The compulsion that you use to hide the pain gets to the point where it gets bigger than you and it starts running away with you. And you end up in deep alcoholism, deep drugs, or locked up in work. I've seen business executives just as deep in work as any skid row alcoholic is in wine. I know because I was far enough gone that it took a two-week vacation for me to get quieted down so that the last few days of it I started to be able to see my predicament. If I had kept on going like I was without a heart attack, I would have just gone off into outer space. The person with the work compulsion like me gets to the point where their only reason for living is their job. And guys particularly are in this bag. And what's the average longevity? The average longevity is something like sixty-five years and eleven months. If they live, they retire at sixty-five and then eleven months later they're dead.

I used to think there were all kinds of legitimate life styles—to each his own. And that's true in one sense. If each of us did what was right for us we would each be so

29

unique you could tell us apart from a mile away. But our individual life styles don't reflect our uniqueness. Four or five common patterns cover most everybody. It should be 200 million individual life styles. Those limited, rigid life styles of ours reflect the way we play God and try to control ourselves and life and botch up the job. As our control systems start to break down, we should see their fruitlessness and give them up. But we don't. We just try harder and harder at something that's failed so in the past. And so we get deeper into our compulsions.

There is nothing wrong with what we make a compulsion of. Alcohol, drugs, work, sex, and power are all lovely things when used the right way. But when a person tries to use one of those beautiful things to run away from his or her emotional pain, then it starts being a compulsion. And the compulsion gets worse and worse. As the compulsion gets a deeper hold and becomes an addiction, it stops giving any satisfaction, but the person is trapped and can't get out of the compulsion until he or she is finally ready to ask for and accept help.

I see now that it makes no sense justifying a compulsion as part of a legitimate life style. Sure a person can be an alcoholic if he wants to. That's his business. But it doesn't make sense for me to have a compulsion and justify it as being good for me. How can it be good for me to be a slave to my habit, whether it's drugs or something socially acceptable like work or power? An addiction is an addiction.

I believe I was meant to be a creative outgoing personality and I believe everybody else was meant to be creative and outgoing, too. By outgoing I don't mean a noisy backslapper. I mean being able to express myself when it is appropriate, like being able to show someone I love them instead of being withdrawn and inhibited.

So I think that each of us needs exactly the right life style, but I can't see how any of those life styles include compulsions that we hang on to. Sure I've got my compulsions, but I'm doing everything I can and I'm asking for the help of my higher power to scale down or remove those compulsions as fast as I can.

How come I made life as miserable for myself as a person could make it? If you would have said to me, "Jess, you figure out a system as absolutely miserable as you possibly can," I couldn't in my wildest dreams have figured out a system as lousy as that. No conscious mind would be that ingenious or that fiendish to devise such a torture chamber.

Okay, how did I bring it about? I get kind of amused now when students come to me and they have this litany of their parents' sins. "Jess, you can't believe how lousy I was raised. My ma was a hard-shell Baptist and boy, she poured fundamental religion into me. She was pure hypocrite. She lied, drank, cheated and stole, and ran around with the neighbors' husbands and yet she preached hard-shell Baptist to me. No wonder I'm screwed up." And then the next student would come and say, "Jess, you wouldn't believe our house. We had a complete absence of contact. Nobody told me to do nothing and that's why I'm so bad. I was just let run loose."

More and more I've seen that my own parental complaints are minuscule compared to those gigantic ones various people would trot into my office with. People would tell me, "Why everybody that I remember as a kid told me I was lousy and no good. No wonder I turned out the way I did." And I thought, "Gee, there were a lot of people in my childhood besides my parents who thought I was a pretty nice little kid. And they were nice to me. It

31

must have been terrible to have grown up the way they did."

When I got a clearer picture of how insane I had really become, I realized I had done many of those insane things to myself without the help of a lot of extenuating circumstances. I had a good father and a good mother. I had a couple of wonderful grandparents, who took a big hand in raising me. I had a lot of people in my little town who liked me and looked after me and took an interest in me. I didn't have a perfect childhood by a long shot, but mine wasn't enough worse than many others to account for all my problems. So I did practically all of this to myself, unaided by other people.

How come? I think it's simple. I was born with the natural and normal self-protective mechanisms that I think every child has. And I went out into the world and it was too big for me. It was too complicated. It was too overwhelming. I had the same problem I suspect perhaps everybody else had, and that was that I was not big enough for life. I was childish and self-centered. As I got a few assaults on my puny little ego, I became more and more locked up in self, more and more anxious to make a bunch of big ego scenes that would make the world see me as I wanted to be seen, to keep the world away or handle it on my terms.

When J. J. Walker of "Good Times" got an award on television a while back he said, "Here comes the Black Prince." Well, I was the White Prince, only nobody was giving me my kingdom and nobody was bowing down to me. I wanted the whole world to be run on my terms, on my time schedule, for me. I wanted it to be sunny today so I could be on a picnic. I wanted it to be sunny tomorrow so I could walk to the store in the sunshine. I wanted it to be sunny the following day because I didn't want it to be gloomy when I got up in the morning. If you would have had me running the weather, the crops would have burned up and the plants would have just shriveled up and died.

I was so completely lost in self that I wanted everything to revolve around me personally. Everything that happened, I took personally. And most everything that happened wasn't the way I wanted it, so it was an affront to me. I was continually crying out, "Why does this have to happen to me?"

I've seen suffering. Some of it is inevitable in life. We will meet it and handle it as well as we can. And it will pass and the sun will shine for us again. But most of the suffering in my life came to be a very precious signal to me that I was doing something wrong. And it took me so much pain, so often, to learn that there is an order and harmony, a lawfulness, in that world out there. It is not all madness.

Say some little guy in a green suit came down here from Mars and he wanted to get around in this world. He would need a car. He would need to know how to drive. And say you taught him how to drive but you played a trick on him. You told him, "Hey, I'll teach you how to run this car, how to start it and how to stop it. But I'm not going to tell you how to live in the world of drivers. I'm going to let you find out for yourself." You give him only one clue. "What those drivers are doing out there, despite appearances to the contrary, is orderly. There is some order in what those drivers are doing. Your job is to discover what that order is."

What would he discover? He would discover that by and large people drive on the right side of the road. By and large, when lights are green, people go ahead and when they are red they stop, by and large. So he finds there is a set of universal laws which are respected, by and large. Once he had that one clue, that there was orderliness out there, it wouldn't take him long to figure out the system.

What kind of driver am I? Simple. I drive the wrong way down one-way streets with my eyes shut. A lot of people tell me, "Jess, God gives me all these clues that I'm doing wrong." Well, maybe their God works that way, but my God doesn't need to send me all kinds of messages because when I shut my eyes as I'm going down the freeway of life and my tires start bouncing some, is that God stepping down and giving me a clue something is wrong? No, that is the rough road on the shoulder of the highway telling me through my tires that something is wrong. God doesn't need to do anything. The ditch and its roughness are already there. Having my eyes closed doesn't change anything. But say I continue to ignore the signs in my hardheaded Norwegian way. What happens? Pretty soon I get some real shocks to the front end of my car. What are those shocks? That's me and my car wiping out fence posts. Pretty soon I get this gigantic lurch and that's me starting to go off a rocky cliff into a deep lake.

Those are the kind of signals life sends me when my little car of life is off the road. The suffering and pain I get, most of it, is a very precious clue that I'm doing something wrong. You may object. You may say, "That implies I'm doing something wrong. I've never done anything wrong, I'm the White Prince. Oh, sure, one time I talked back to a bartender but that was only because I had too much to drink and wasn't myself. But that's the only wrong thing I ever did." Well, is that so? Then we'll let the laws of life hand you a little more pain because you obviously haven't learned anything yet.

Now that's not very pretty news for any of us in one

sense but it is in another. If the world is a terrible place, then you and I can't change it. But if what we see in the world that makes us think it's terrible is coming out of our self-centeredness, then that's better because we have some chance of changing our self-centeredness. And this is what I've seen through my work with Alcoholics Anonymous. I'm not an alcoholic but I've seen through groups like AA that people who are the most destructive to themselves and to the people around them all of a sudden start changing their behavior and the world starts smoothing out. I see now that the world doesn't need to change. It's all right the way it is. But *I* need to change.

I spent the earlier years of my life with one of the worst groups of malcontents the world has ever seen, the college intellectuals. To most college intellectuals, absolutely nothing is right except themselves. Everything else is wrong. Their whole lives are spent searching out all the different problems of the world and understanding them in tremendous detail so that they can talk knowledgeably with all their fellow intellectuals and wring their hands in horror and pose their instant solutions.

I was that college intellectual, but I see now that the world in a way is just about exactly the opposite of how I used to look at it back in those days when I was so terribly smart.

I have come to see that there is a tremendous, beautiful harmony in life. I have come to see that even with my limited understanding there is an immense amount of beauty and smoothness and fitness within the system. The reason I couldn't see it before was because I was in the center. I was like a spoiled child lying on the floor kicking his heels and screaming because his mommy wouldn't let him eat the whole batch of cookies. I wanted things my way. I wanted them on my time. And I gave no thought to the consequences for anyone else. My tremendous, almost complete self-centeredness was the major problem that I had.

I see now that the more I can get out of the center the better, because this world does not revolve around me. The more I can get out of the center, the better things go, and the more order and harmony there is for me.

It is just like in the old days when they believed the sun revolved around the earth. They came up with a bunch of astronomical laws that didn't work very well. You have to make all those special exceptions to the laws. But the minute they realized they and their precious earth weren't the center of the world and that the earth revolved around the sun, then the new astronomical laws they could figure out were all orderly, and they didn't need to make all the special exceptions. There were very few gaps in their knowledge.

I find it's the same way with life. When I'm in the center, nothing goes right. When I'm out of the center, most everything smooths out. More and more I've come to feel that's probably why life was given to me, so I could learn that. My whole lifetime, as near as I can see, I will spend learning that one lesson. But I can't think of anything more important to concentrate on. From the small progress I have made at getting out of the center, I've already reaped some very, very rich rewards.

When I'm in the center and asking life to revolve around me, I'm being God. When I stop being God, that's the first step in accepting some power outside myself. I'm not the one who's in charge of making the sun come up. My job isn't to wake up each morning ahead of sunrise, tell the sun, "Okay, sun, get up now," and take a big lever and pry the sun above the horizon. Some other power, some power greater than myself, takes care of things like that. That way I can sleep later in the morning. And rest easier.

It's like life is a merry-go-round. I spent most of my early years pushing the merry-go-round. It was very hard work and I was tremendously envious and angry at all these people who were sitting riding their horses in the breeze, having such a lovely time, and I was doing all the work. Then one day, in my dull Norwegian mind, I finally realized the merry-go-round had a motor and I didn't need to push the merry-go-round. If anything, it would go a little faster if I would stop holding it back, and it could go more smoothly. I could then go and get on the pretty dapple gray horse with a companion of my choice and have a lovely time riding in the breeze.

Then I found that the merry-go-round made pretty music. But I hadn't been able to hear the music before because I was working so hard pushing the merry-go-round that my heavy breathing drowned out the music. So finally in life I could begin to say to my companion on the merry-go-round, "Ain't I a wonder . . . and ain't you a wonder, too?" But having a good time riding the merry-go-round makes me feel a little guilty. Who is going to be the great fixer-upper of the world? I don't get out of this God business easy. If I'm not fixing up all the world's problems, like starvation in Africa, who could possibly do it? I know all of the three billion other people on earth can't conceivably see and care about some of the problems in the world they way I do. Obviously, only I have sufficient concern and sufficient incentive, because obviously everyone else in the world is a hopeless derelict without the compassion and wisdom that I possess.

So I feel guilty sitting there on the merry-go-round going up and down in the breeze having a lovely time because I'm not doing what I should be doing, which is fixing things up. So how can I handle that feeling?

I need to see another thing. I need to see this world is a lovely place. But for this old, hard-core college intellectual to say, "Hey, the world is a lovely place," is terribly, terribly hard and I don't know if I'll ever make it. I can see it a little better now though.

In my first book I talked about the necessity of acceptance. But to me that's not anywhere's near the right word for it any more. The word is all right as far as it goes, but when we say acceptance, there's so much grudgingness implied and often even a lack of approval. "I must accept you but I don't need to approve of you." It's acceptance through gritted teeth. That kind of acceptance isn't worth much.

So what I've come to see is that we need, not a partial acceptance, but an absolute acceptance of these things in life, and unless we can manage that it means we're still in the God business. I need to go way beyond acceptance. I need to get to where I can literally embrace the world. As one of my students said long ago: "I have taken a tremendous bite from the apple of life—and found it green but sweet."

I have come to see that contentment isn't in circumstances. A lot of people have said to me, "Jess, you've really got it whipped. You're living in this pretty mountain valley just outside Bozeman. You've got your horses, and skiing, and what have you. If I was living like you I would have no problems. But here I am trapped in this city or that city. And the kids are stealing the batteries of my car and cutting the cables. If I was living in that pure air like you instead of breathing the polluted air of St. Paul, it would be different."

But the answer is no, it wouldn't be different. Montana's

suicide rate is higher than yours. It is not quite as high as the suicide rate for some professions like dentists, but it is higher than the suicide rate in most industrial states.

So I've come to see that contentment is not something that you find; contentment is something that comes to you when you and I are ready to open the door to it and let it into our hearts and our lives. It's inside us waiting to be discovered. But, all in all, it is me being God that blocks this process and keeps contentment out. Let's look at how we can stop being God, get our heads out of our navels, get out of the center, and get in harmony with life. That way we can all be riding the merry-go-round with a lovely companion, feeling the sweet cool breeze on our faces and listening to the lovely music of the calliope.

TWO

I Don't Know How to Love Me—
Self-acceptance

The few people I've met who were happy with themselves weren't made any differently than anyone else. They were just reasonably happy with the way they were made and their faces and bodies showed it. Their faces were relaxed and content, and their bodies were at ease.

I see now that all happiness, peace, contentment, and serenity for me starts with self-acceptance. If I want more peace and happiness in my life, then I need to be more accepting of myself.

Somewhere back there in my early days, I felt inadequate. I could feel things weren't going right and in my childish mind I thought that meant there was something wrong with me. As I became more and more afraid of what I was, I had to pretend to be something I wasn't.

There's a person you and I never get away from our whole life long. That person is ourselves. You'd think if we were going to live our whole life with someone, we would want him to be a friend. But unfortunately most of us live, not with a friend, but with a person we hate, despise, and fear. That hated, despised, feared person is ourselves. Very few people I've ever met were completely happy with the way they were made. Most had some things or many things about themselves they couldn't stand and they wanted to change as quickly as they could. And the pain and sadness and fear they felt was written all over their faces.

I felt I had to build a high wall around myself so people couldn't look in and discover what I was really like. In the process of hiding my inner self from you, I also hid it from me and I built higher and higher walls against the only people who could save my life—the people around me.

I recently had a very beautiful experience that showed me how different life can be. I walked into a group I have been close to for many years. All of us in that group had opened our hearts to each other week after week. For the first time, I didn't feel that some were men and some were women, they were all just human hearts. That was a beautiful feeling for me when I briefly transcended these dumb distinctions, sexual and otherwise, that we have. Because a pretty girl isn't a pretty girl, she's just a heart with a pretty face on the outside and an ugly girl isn't an ugly girl, she is just a heart with a face on the outside and the heart is what counts. So all women are beautiful and all men are beautiful.

Most of the time I can't realize that because of my limitations as a person and my self-centeredness and my egotism. When I was in college I'd occasionally date these beautiful gals so I could walk in and the guys would say, "Wow, look what he got." And all this gal wanted to talk about was how many angora sweaters she had. I tell you, a date with her seemed like it lasted forever. After one night with her, I said, "Hey, it ain't worth it. It ain't worth suffering like that to knock the guys' eyes out."

Finally, after thirty-five years of lying to myself, my little car went off the road of life into the ditch and hit a huge, gigantic rock. My heart attack woke me up a lot because I finally admitted, "Hey, I'm off the road. I'm out of harmony with life. I think I should do something about it or I won't go any further." And my little car was smashed against a rock, demolished. So I said to life, "Okay, I'll go back to the road. I'll hitchhike and try to find my way."

When I had that heart attack and was lying in the emergency room I had a beautiful, beautiful moment of calm. I was able to quietly understand, "My God, in most everything I've done, I've made the wrong decision, and taken a whole bunch of wrong turns in my life. I've gotten further and further away from what I really believe in deep down to the point where I'm not doing anything I believe in." I vowed to myself, "I'm never again going to do anything I don't believe in." And that's got to be the single most beautiful thing that's ever happened to me. That experience was a spiritual awakening. I had had spiritual awakenings before, but afterward I had gone right back to sleep, right back to the old ways, not much changed by what had happened.

I remember when I was young and in college. I came down the sawdust trail in the Methodist church hollering, "I repent. No more am I going to be a sinner." It was on a Sunday night I was saved and I had all these hopes and wonderful feelings and I felt a new life in me. I went right down to the Marigold Ballroom and told the guys, "I'm not going to hang around with sinners like you any more, dancing with these gals and holding them close. I'm not going to do that any more."

You know where I was the next Sunday night? That is how long that spiritual awakening lasted. The next Sunday night I was back at the Marigold Ballroom holding those gals very close.

Now there's nothing wrong with spiritual awakenings and the spirit. The spirit's a wonderful thing. It is just dealing with an awful hard case when it's dealing with me. That's a very powerful spirit but in me it had a tough nut to crack.

In the years before my heart attack I knew that what I was doing wasn't what I believed in but I didn't always know what it was that I believed in. There were times when I practically had to flip a coin to see which of two things I should do.

As I was lying in the hospital one of the things I knew I didn't believe in was going back to the career I had been chasing—being an advertising man. I sold my agency on the telephone. There's nothing wrong with the advertising business, but it was sure wrong for me. I was scared stiff most of the time. And most of the people around me seemed to be just as scared as I was because advertising didn't seem to fit them either. I saw so much fear around me in advertising that I thought there was a lot of fear in every career.

I started asking people around me, "Hey, what do you think I should be? What do you think I am?" Before my question had been, "What am I going to do to make a lot of money?" When I started going to the University of Minnesota, I didn't know what I wanted to be. I took an aptitude test and they said, "You should be an advertising man or an engineer." I said, "To hell with the wheels, I'll take the people." And I became an advertising man so I

43

could make $75,000 a year and really show people I was something.

I was like the old cowboy in Montana who, each Saturday night, walked into the saloon, plunked his money down on the bar, and shouted, "Let's get drunk and be somebody." That poor, dumb guy didn't know he already was somebody and he was in the process of becoming a lot less somebody than he was when he started out.

My goal was to make $75,000 a year. That was back in 1949 when that was even a lot more money than it is today. I was going to make $75,000 a year and really show somebody I was something just like the drunken cowboy. But I had life backwards.

A guy named Wally Minto of Alpha Awareness training in Susanville, California, has a tape called "Results" and it's a most startling thing. He sure spells out in his tape why I was getting such poor results. I was going to *have* a big income and a big house and a fancy deal. I would *do* what I had to do to have that. And then I would *be* what I had to *be* to *do* what I had to *do* to *have* that big income. I was starting with HAVING and then DOING and only last BEING.

Now that's just exactly backwards as Wally Minto so beautifully points out. The universe flows in the opposite direction. The great stream of life flows the other way. It goes from BEING to DOING to HAVING and I was spending my time swimming upstream. And you don't swim very fast when you try to swim against the current, especially someone with the very limited physical equipment that I've got. Some people make a success of swimming upstream for most of their lives, or at least it's what they think of as a success. And they never have the experience of having a heart attack and finding there's another way.

44

I changed around and went with the stream of life. It's not all that difficult; we see it all the time in the folks who go into AA. Once a person comes out of his alcoholism and decides he can't be anyone but himself, he starts doing whatever is appropriate to his being and then he ends up having whatever is appropriate to that being and that doing. It is just breathtaking when you see alcoholics come up out of the depths, even off skid row. It's like my old friend says: "One minute they're looking for a can to cook-up in and after they come into AA they start looking for a place to park their Cadillac." And that Cadillac isn't bought on time.

It isn't everybody who gets Cadillacs in AA, but most everybody in AA soon gets prosperity in the sense of having more money than they're spending, mostly because they aren't spending with both hands to dull their emotional pain. I've never been addicted to alcohol. It doesn't do anything for me except put me to sleep. But I've sure learned a lot from those people I've met who are in Alcoholics Anonymous.

So I changed around and decided to go with the stream of life. I said, "I'm going to accept myself as I am." And then I took a look at the package and I started to gulp as I got a clearer picture of what it was I was letting myself in for. I used to think I was a very sensitive person; what I found out was I was a touchy bastard. If you didn't handle me with kid gloves, I got mad. If you didn't stroke my feathers in just exactly the right direction at the right tempo with the right gentleness, I took offense. If the people sitting in the audience didn't look just right, I'd get mad and upset. I defended myself by saying I was just being sensitive. But I wasn't sensitive, I was just touchy and I had to look at that touchiness in me and say, "Is that me?" and the answer was, "Yeah, that's me."

I had to see my limitations. It's amazing to me all the things I can't do. I can't walk on water, but I want to. I want the whole world to love me. "Please don't argue with me, anybody, ever." I don't like that. I want to be right all of the time to the point where I want everybody to say, "My God, I've never heard anybody as right as you. You're just right all the time, aren't you?"

And I had to see my strengths. I had to see, "Hey, on my good days, occasionally, I can do something halfway decent." That's a big problem for me to admit because then I'm responsible for what I do once in a while instead of always being able to excuse myself and fall into self-pity. "Oh, woe is me. Who can expect anything out of poor little old me." Hopeless and helpless, that's me. I'm like the girl who doesn't have a hope chest; she has a hopeless chest because she just knows nobody would want to marry anyone as ugly as her. But what she's got is external beauty mixed up with internal beauty. She's actually pretty but she can't admit that to herself.

When I started to come out of myself a little, I started meeting people who brought up some ideas I found very difficult to handle. One of the points they raised was the question of my sanity. I wanted to hit them. I said, "That doesn't apply to me. Insane people are the ones who are locked up. Insanity, that doesn't apply to me. After a while I could see, "Maybe it applies a little, but it's too strong a word." But by now I've come to see insanity is just the right word for what I was. If anything, it's a little too mild for someone who nearly succeeded in killing himself with a heart attack at thirty-five and wasn't doing anything he believed in, and was spending his whole life trying to impress people he didn't even like.

What do you call one who has carefully constructed a torture chamber and calls it love, whose whole purpose of life is to kill himself? And even worse than that, who is making his life, until he dies, murderously painful? If you were going to put labels on what I just described it would be something to the effect of an absolute 100 per cent raving maniacal insanity with delusions of grandeur and all kinds of other words for twisted and warped perceptions. When I saw that about myself I finally saw that I needed to be restored to some degree of sanity.

As I was running down this roster of myself, I then had to face some of the things I had done when I was so caught up in self. I had to take a searching and fearless moral inventory of myself. The first time was really hard because I had to say, "Hey, I talked back to that bartender one time, I sometimes sang too loud in church, and I hit a slush puddle with my car and showered an old man one time." Oh, I did some terrible things. And once I got those terrible things out of the way, then I could get down to what was really wrong. I was 10 per cent caught up in self-centered, egotistical acting. That's all. I was cruel, harmful, and neglectful, first of all to myself and all the people I claimed to love, and secondly to all the rest of the world. That's all. Those are just little things, you know.

As I told these things to another human being, I got some relief. And I got rid of a lot of skeletons that were hidden in my closet. One of the first sexual things I got off my chest, I told to a gal who came in to see me. She was telling me that even though she was engaged to a guy in California she was spending a lot of time horizontal in Montana. And this bothered her because she didn't think that gals who were engaged were supposed to be horizontal with guys so much. She was even taking birth control pills regularly.

When she said, "What does this say about me, Jess?" I

47

said, "Hey, Sandy, it says you are a member of the human race." I was looking for some sexual thing of mine that was troubling to me. And I told her about the time when I was baptized at twelve in a big tank by immersion. I came up the steps out of the tank having just been saved in the name of the Father and the Son and the Holy Ghost. Dorothy Black came up behind me with that white dress just sticking to her with every detail of her body revealed. I had all kinds of sinful thoughts. I thought, "My God, here I am standing at the altar having these terrible thoughts."

What I find is that when a person starts taking a searching and fearless moral inventory, a lot of times sexual stuff is chief among the things that are bothering them. But I find once we get the skeletons out in the open, whatever they are, it's like pulling the cork in the bottle. Once the cork is out, we can get at the real problem. And the real problem is always ourselves and the things we do each day.

There is an interesting contrast in the two major views of the cause of neurosis. One view is that our neurosis comes from impulses or actions of a much earlier time, like when we wanted to push Pa out of bed and sleep with Ma and we feel bad because we had the thought. Maybe we didn't even know we had the thought. The other view of neurosis is that we feel terrible about some of the awful things we did to people yesterday. I believe this bothers us a lot more. Until we stop doing those things to the people around us, we won't stop feeling bad. We have a problem here, though, because we won't admit to ourselves the awful things we are doing. So until we are able to get halfway honest with ourselves, we can't see where our trouble is coming from. We think we are such lovely people that we just wouldn't do anything bad. Yesterday we were just giving those other people what they deserved. But I see that as people become more honest, they can see the awful things they are doing to themselves and to others. As they stop doing such harmful things in their yesterdays, they feel much better in their todays.

I saw a nun at the airport when I was coming home from Minneapolis a while ago. The nun was first in line for flight check-in and she had a lady friend who was helping her. The agent put up his seating chart, took off about ten seating stickers, and put them aside. Because I'm ten times as cantankerous as the nun, I knew what she was going to say and do before she did it, which made it harder for me when she did it. She said through gritted teeth, "If you keep taking all those stickers off there won't be any place for me to sit." He told her he was taking stickers off because there were ten people who had been in the plane when it landed and were continuing on the flight. He asked her if she wanted smoking or non-smoking and the smoke came out of her ears. She said, "Non-smoking," and took her stuff away. She sat down at the end of a row of seats and filled up the next two seats besides with her coat and bags so the lady with the nun had to sit three seats away. The nun dragged out her knitting and started knitting furiously. I heard the lady with the nun ask her something about her knitting and the nun said, "Oh, a sweater like this with cable stitch is much more stimulating than straight knitting." That was three minutes in a nun's life and it wouldn't have hurt so much if it all wasn't so familiar to me. That nun was like the hatchery trout planted in the stream. Like me, she was causing all kinds of commotion for herself and the people around her. And then at the end of the day I'm sure she wondered what it was in her distant past that made her hurt so much. Yet I think most of her answer was in her daily life, if she could only open her eyes and see honestly what she was doing.

As I go through life, so much of the time my message is, "World give me what I want, world get out of my way, people don't touch me, don't disturb my self-centered self." After twenty-four hours of living like that, of course I'm in pain. Why should I have to look back to my early years for a cause? That's like a guy sitting in his house and it's burning down. He smells smoke and thinks, "Hmm, I smell smoke. There must be forest fires burning up in Canada this summer."

All my stories on me and the one on the nun show you why I believe my neurosis comes from what I did yesterday. At the very root of the problem is my self-centeredness. In my egotism I make myself a god. As a kid I had some very fine religious training by very nice people in a quiet way. Nobody beat on me. But on my own I changed the commandments around. When Christ Himself was asked about which of the commandments Moses brought us was the greatest, Christ said, in essence, Love the Lord with all thy heart and all thy soul and all thy mind and love thy neighbor as thyself. But I said Christ didn't know what he was doing. He should have answered differently. He should have said there are really two important commandments of the ten; you shouldn't steal and the sex commandment. Those are the two big commandments. As long as you don't violate them in any obvious way that catches the attention of the neighbors, then you're all right.

I was playing God and I was rewriting religion to suit myself so I could look good. Those two commandments, in their very literal interpretation, I could keep. For one thing, if all your energies are focused so hard in your business there isn't much extra energy looking for a sexual outlet. It's like Vince says: "If staying away from sex would have made me a saint, they could have crowned me St. Vince, because when I got deep enough in wine, there wasn't any sex left." So I was playing God, you see, by rewriting religion. I could pretend I lived up to religion's laws yet go my own way in everything else but sex and stealing.

I now see that there are only three grievous sins I commit and they are the ones in the great commandment. I don't even need to be a Christian to see that the first of them is playing God, putting some other god before God. I made myself a god. I made money a god, and I made a god out of what people thought about me. The other two most grievous sins are not loving my neighbor or myself.

Well, what kind of rule is that where you're going to be breaking it all the time. Help! It makes me want to go back to that nice clean deal I had before, where I would go for months and years without stealing money or jumping in bed with the neighbor's wife. Then I was clean. I had a nice, clear, certain feeling that I was being a very good little boy.

A fine man, Reverend Bruce Morgan, calls this making religion into little boxes. And this world is too big to be put into neat little boxes. The uncertainty of the law of love makes living it nearly impossible. We see it's impossible to be right under that system, so in our fear we try to narrow things down so we make a nice egotistic set of boxes. We strip our religion down to a little set of boxes and we try to live in them. We say, "I don't break this rule and that rule and the other rule so I can go around saying "Hallelujah" and look what a beautiful person I am." Bruce calls that "dead" religion. It doesn't work. Don't get me wrong here. I don't want to talk religion. I'm talking about a set of teachings that came out of a

51

specific religion, but they are alarmingly like the teachings of every other religion I've ever looked at also. And even more so, you don't need to have any religion to see how these ideas work.

And don't care if you ever adopt any religion. Most people I see in AA don't have any formal religion any more because they got so burned on it they never went back. And then once they get into AA they see enough harmony and get enough understanding of the spiritual well enough that they don't really see the need for something else. In fact, they can't get what they need out of a lot of the dead religions.

It's just like the little green guy from Mars who we were going to teach how to drive. You go out in life and you find these principles are out there and you don't need to call them any religious name. These principles aren't just revealed to certain people and written down. They are like gravity. Gravity is universal. It doesn't work for some and not others. Gravity is out in the open for all of us to see. All we need to do is look. Same way with the principles I'm talking about here. They are out there for anyone to see and experience and establish as true to his or her own satisfaction.

Put no other gods before you. You know what that is? That's the same idea as the merry-go-round story. When I found the merry-go-round had a motor was when I realized the world does not revolve around me. I am not in the center, thank God, I am not the center. When I am at the center, my life breaks down at the center. This life has a center. It has a harmony. There is a power greater than myself. I now see that if I can't admit there's something bigger than me that takes care of getting the sun up while I sleep, then I'm crazy. So what I've been struggling to do is to see what I truly am, to find my being and accept that being so I can get in Harmony with life.

If I'm not going to be God, then I don't need to be perfect, because the only thing that is absolutely perfect is God. That's the definition of God in any system. If I don't need to be perfect, then my imperfections don't need to trouble me so much. In fact, they are a very great advantage to me. Why? Because they say I don't need to be God. So then my imperfections are all of a sudden working for me instead of working against me. That means all of a sudden they're a lot easier to look at because my imperfections are what confirm my humanity. They're my ticket to allow me to ride on the merry-go-round instead of pushing it.

At first, I found it very difficult to admit to my God, to myself, and to another human being the exact nature of my wrongs. I've been doing that continuously ever since I found the importance of doing it the first time. And now there isn't anything I've ever done or felt troubled about that I haven't told at least one person and often many.

Some people argue it's enough to admit your imperfections to yourself, to your God, and to your priest. I tried that and it didn't give me any relief. Most Catholics I see would rather go to the dentist than go to confession. And when they do go to confession, so many make childish little confessions like I did, telling about missing Mass and prayers and being angry at their wives or children. They are afraid to go deep inside to what's really bothering them. They don't want the priest to know about that. Yet I find people who have admitted their imperfections to an intimate friend they could trust feel a great relief, and they are anxious to do it again the minute they see something that has been really bothering them.

I think the reason it makes so much difference to ad-

53

mit our imperfections, shortcomings, and wrongs to another human being is that way we can see the expression on their faces. When I first started telling people some of the awful things I had felt and done, I expected them to draw back in horror, even run from me. Yet no one was ever shocked or surprised. Most of the time I felt a little let down because they didn't react at all to what I thought was some horrible deed or feeling. And some of the times people were close to yawning at what, I can now see, were my puny, little fears. But I had to see this acceptance for what I had done on people's faces to believe it. Without seeing it on their faces, my feeling would have been, "You can say what I've done is all right only because you don't really know me." Most of the people I talk to feel the same way I did. So I see that the only way I can be free of my distorted and overblown fears of what I've done and what I am is to get them out in the open by telling them to an intimate friend I can trust.

Is this putting my burden on another? No. I've never felt burdened by people who tell me how they feel about themselves. I always feel the opposite. I feel better because I see "Here's another person just like me. I'm less alone in my screwed-up thinking and living." I'm not talking about the person who complains about their troubles. They aren't telling you about their honest feelings about themselves or how they feel about another person. I'm talking about saying how we really feel about ourselves, our wrongs against others and our imperfections. To me that's giving the very deepest part of ourselves, the most valuable gift we can give. And it's just the opposite of telling someone else how good we are, how Christian we are, how rich we are, or what's wrong with someone else.

As we dig stuff out of our past, we clean out the subconscious. It's like taking a splinter out of your hand. The hurt soon goes away once the splinter is out. When I told that story to Sandy about me being baptized, I was freed of something that had been lurking there in my subconscious mind bothering me for years. It's like being in a fishing boat with your subconscious mind the water. All the bad deeds and feelings are like corks. You've got a croquet mallet and as a cork pops to the surface you hit it and it goes down a ways. Then another one comes to the top and you hit it. You spend all your time hitting corks, knocking them back down under so you don't need to see them. The only thing is you don't have energy for anything else but hitting corks and it's very tiring.

So I say, "Okay, I'm going to put my croquet mallet in the boat and I'm going to let the corks come to the surface. Then I'm going to take each cork and say, 'Hey, look at that.' And the person I'm talking to listens and laughs. When I asked the typist what she thought about the story I had told Sandy when she handed me back the transcript of a tape I had made of it, she said, "Oh, I thought that was cute. When we were in the Lutheran choir, we had those big white robes and they were awful hot in the summer time and we didn't wear much underneath them. The guys would try to maneuver around to get the sun behind us so they could see through our gowns."

At first I didn't think my confession was funny. That was what I had been spending so much energy on trying to push it out of my mind all these years, because that memory made me feel so horrible it conflicted with my self-centered ideal of what I was supposed to be, which is perfect. Perfect people don't do things like that. They have only beautiful thoughts and everything is lovely and it is a beautiful world with everybody doing beautiful things for beautiful people.

But I've gone on since then getting rid of the skeletons in my closet. I thought I had it all cleaned out but about six months ago I realized there was something that had been bothering me a long time. I ran and told somebody I could trust real quick so I didn't have any more energy invested in that cork. I suppose there are a few more corks submerged down there but the minute one of them comes up I'm going to find an intimate friend I can trust and tell them about it. That drains away the hold that memory has on me. It isn't a problem any more.

After I had admitted my defects of character, I was faced with a new problem. I had to be entirely ready to be freed of all these defects of character. I got to the point, after I started looking at this mess of myself long enough, where I thought, "My God, if you took away my defects of character, there wouldn't be anything left. I'd just be a hollow shell." As I looked at myself more honestly I began to feel that all I was was defects of character and nothing else. I thought, "My God, if you took away my defects of character, what would I do with my time? How would I fill up my days?" I began to see, though, that there might be some other reasonable uses for that time.

Finally, after a long period of time, I was ready to be freed of my defects of character and I humbly asked my higher power to remove my shortcomings. One of the first things my higher power took away was something that I didn't think was a defect of character. I thought it was a strong part of my personality. The thing that was changed was the way I taught. I had been walking into the classroom and saying, "Here is a pound of Jess Lair. Don't you like it? If you don't, I'll squish it around some way to make you like it. I know I can make you like it.

Hang on. Don't leave. Don't leave, please! I'm sure I can find some way to make you like me."

I thought that desire to please others was a good thing about me. As a teacher, it had helped me to be king of the St. Paul campus of the University of Minnesota. It made me a very popular teacher. But talk about plastic, that was me. I was like Silly Putty that you can make into any shape. "If you don't like me this way, let me try it some other way." And I thought that was a strength. My higher power, whom I choose to call God, took that away.

Another problem I had was that I was very careful with my money—some would say stingy. It was all right if I spent a lot on me. But I didn't want to spend too much on the wife and the kids. If you give money to your wife, all she does is waste it on food. And when it came to giving the kids their allowances, I was really tight. I would buy some big things for them that I could take credit for. I'd buy them a pair of skis so they could say, "Dad bought me skis." But give them a nickel?, what credit is there in that for me? What's pleasing my ego about that? Nothing. So let the wife give them their allowance and the nickels and the dollars. And when you hand out nickels and dollars the way things cost today and with all things needed at school, man you tear an awful hole in the budget as all of you know so well.

So my wife was shucking money out of her pocket for the kids. I was writing her a check each month and she was shucking it out so she had to endure the pain. Then I could say, "What are you doing with all your money?" Isn't that beautiful? That's the way you save money. And someone in the house has got to be saving like me.

I came to see, "Hey, maybe that isn't the best system. I had watched old Vince dish out money to his kids just as easy as could be. So I started trying to hand out money. It nearly killed me. And it nearly killed my kids. They almost died of shock. That was a couple of years ago. But it's getting better. Recently my wife, in a kidding way, said something to the kids to the effect of "Well, see if your stingy old man will give this to you." And one of the boys said, "Stingy? Dad?" That just shows how fast a kid can forget.

Near as I can see most of my defects of character are still painfully in place and glaringly obvious to you, waiting for me to get ready to give them up. Or they are waiting for my higher power to decide he's going to take them away. Or they are waiting for me to understand they aren't defects of character, they are strong supporting columns of my personality. But that's not my business. Some things I can change, like my stinginess, but I'm not in the business of changing my basic personality. If I could change my personality, think of my ego. My job as I see it, deals with acceptance. I have to come to a complete acceptance of what can't be changed or what hasn't been changed yet. Now I know five years from now I'm going to be a somewhat different person than I am today in some of my specific characteristics. I will be given the courage to change some things and I will probably have some more little spiritual awakenings or changes in my basic personality.

One of my friends from the past, Bob Schmitt, was kind of angry about the book my wife and I wrote, *"Hey, God, What Should I Do Now?"* That book told of the events of our life from our two different points of view. "Jess," he said, "you haven't changed a bit. You're still the same hard-charging, mean, cantankerous, ornery person you always were. And now you are creating this phony impression with people. You're telling them how different you are. That isn't fair." And he was offended. And he was right. Because I am alarmingly like I ever was. And that to me is beautiful.

The way I see our personalities is that deep down inside there is a unique essence that's really us. But our fear of ourselves and of our uniqueness makes us try to be a bunch of things we aren't. And those things we try to be but aren't are the false parts of our personality that are often defects of character or at least aren't needed. As we start to get rid of those things that aren't us, we are left with the unique essence of us. This is the part that doesn't change, that can't change.

What my friend Bob was reacting to was that I am a hard-charging person and I probably always will be. I suspect I may calm down a little but no one will ever find me so loose they mistake me for a wet noodle. So that's what I mean when I say the essence of me never changes. The only problem is I can't know which parts of me are truly me and will stay and which parts are false and will be taken away. Not until something is taken away can I be sure that wasn't a part of the essence of me. So I need to be willing to give up any part of me. I can't decide which parts of me I can and will give up and which parts I won't. I need to surrender, get in harmony with life, and be happy that what isn't needed will be taken away.

I used to wonder how come God made all of you so different from me. And how come God made all of you so different from each other. I couldn't figure out why this world was made up of such different kinds of people. More and more I've come to see the world's that way so there can be a few people who like a nut like me. And it works out just great. That means there are some people who can like each person. And to have that happen there's got to be an awful different bunch of people in this

59

world. As my friend Floyd says, you've got to have a huge pile of wrenches in your tool kit if you're going to have one to fit every nut in the world. So that's how come there are a lot of different people. Thank God I'm so different. And I'm going to stay very much like I am. The only thing I wanted to say to my old friend Bob Schmitt was the cost of being myself has changed drastically. And the people around me now can verify that, plus my doctor can verify that. First of all, I'm alive fifteen years after my heart attack. I had heart surgery and got two extra arteries in my heart ten years ago and they're working like gangbusters. So now I can powder ski at 10,000 feet and elk hunt without overtaxing my heart. Those are the things I can do at fifty. I had to have some improvement or I couldn't do things like that.

I also used to have long depressions where, for a week or two, I'd go to my office and I just couldn't do anything. I'd have an ad to do where, if I didn't meet my deadline, it would cost me a lot of money. And I would cause a lot of pain for my client. But I just couldn't make myself do what I had to do. Now, a long depression for me is half a day and depression doesn't come very often.

There are all kinds of signs in my life things are getting better. I'm not arguing that my life is perfect, but I was happy to get up today. I'm happy to be where I am today and most likely I'm going to be happy where I am tomorrow. And that's how I've changed. I used to get up and have fear all the time. Now I get up without fear and I thank God for my days.

So these are things that I see about self-acceptance. In my first book, *"I Ain't Much, Baby . . ."* I discussed the statement of Carl Rogers which said, "the paradox is that when we accept ourselves as we are, then we can change." I didn't understand, then, how acceptance could work for me but acceptance was the best answer I could see for my problems. Now I think I understand a lot of that statement pretty well and why it is certain to work.

Again, the Wally Minto Alpha Awareness tape gave me a new understanding as to why. First of all he points out what we believe in is what happens. One of the rules this little green Martian guy is going to find out about how the system works, the universal laws, is that what we believe in is going to happen. There's a statement, "As ye believe so shall it be done unto you." And all of this positive thinking is an attempt to try to get in line with that. Only thinking isn't believing. Thinking doesn't go deep enough. Thinking's up in my mind. I've got no problems in the upper story. Up here there's a very calm, logical, rational world. I've got a Ph.D. up here. And I'm using that logical mind to drive my steamboat up the Mississippi River. But there's another guy who's got another set of controls to my boat. He's in a little wheelhouse below me and he's got the doors locked. And that's that subconscious mind, the mind below the top half. And that little devil has a wheel, too. Any time he doesn't want the boat to go the way I'm driving it, he just flips a little switch and turns off my controls and turns on his. And he says, "Let's go put ourselves up on this sandbank for a little while."

I say to myself, "My God, what are we doing? Look! There's a sandbank there. We're going to get hurt. We're going to crash." And sure enough, we do. And I'm turning my wheel like crazy but it's unhooked. I don't have much of a problem with the upper level here, the wheelhouse. It's clean up here and it's all tidy and white with little flowers on the wallpaper. It's a lovely little room up here. But that little devil in that wheelhouse just below me, boy, he lives in a dungeon, let me tell you.

There's stuff down there that would make the Marquis de Sade look like a Sunday-school teacher. The things that guy has got on his mind down there I can just dimly perceive from the places he takes my little boat. And the trouble is that subconscious mind has things under control too much of the time.

Okay, I've got some access to that and one of the things I've seen is that what I fear is what I really, really believe. So when I fear that people will have a bad impression of me, that's what happens. When I fear that people will talk about me in negative and bad ways, that's what happens. When I fear that I will do this and do that, that's what happens.

So the first part of the power of acceptance happens when I say, "That's all right." But you say, "How can you say, that's all right?" We aren't talking about poetry or philosophy here; we are scientists talking about what works. We are talking about being experimental scientists and saying, "Try this out and see if it does work for you because it has sure worked for a lot of other people I know."

So the reason for my honestly looking at my imperfections and the wrongs I do in a day is so I can accept them as me and then say about those things and feelings that they are all right. It is all right that I am a supreme egotist. There are other people who are supreme egotists and they manage to make it through the world. It is all right that I want everybody to love me. It is all right that I'm excessively preoccupied with myself. It is all right that I'm excessively competitive. It is all right that I'm so touchy. It is all right that I'm so cantankerous. It is all right that I'm so arrogant. It is all all right. The minute I say those things about myself are all right, I stop fearing them, I stop fearing them quite a bit—not completely, but quite a bit. And it takes away most of that energy that was wrapped up in that fear, which was bringing about the very things that I feared.

People want to scream at me when I talk like that. They want to say, "Jess, you phony, lousy, rotten cop-out. Do you know what you just did? You just excused yourself from any responsibility for being a decent person at all. How can a person like you be allowed to exist in this world? You should be shot. You're just like someone admitting, 'I'm a robber, a maniac, a killer.' Why we should run and lock you up." The answer is, you're right. The only thing is you're going to have trouble finding a law that's going to help you do it.

But when I say it's all right the way I am, it isn't a cop-out. What it is, it's a way of taking the energy away from all that fear that was bringing about the very things I did today. The person who finally admits he's an alcoholic is a person who's about ready to stop drinking alcohol. An old AA friend of mine was lining up an AA convention and people said to him, "You're not an alcoholic. I've never seen you drink in all the years I've known you." He said, "Oh yeah, I'm an alcoholic."

"Why, that's ridiculous. I thought that guy laying out there in the gutter is an alcoholic."

"Oh, no, he's not an alcoholic," my friend said. "If you don't believe it, just go ask him."

You see the power of acceptance. Fear of something is believing in it and believing helps bring about what you fear.

Another reason acceptance works is simple. I mentioned earlier about Wally Minto's belief that the whole natural order of the universe goes in the opposite way from the way we usually try to go. In my earlier years I was trying to go from having to doing and being. That's backward.

The law of the universe, the whole stream of the universe runs the other way. It runs from BEING to DOING to HAVING. And I hope that all of you in your work are in that work because that's the essential part of your BEING. Then you're DOING what comes logically and inevitably and completely out of the fact that your BEING is to be in that work. And your DOING then is what people in that work inevitably do. And then you will HAVE what people in that work have. And when you are DOING out of a complete sense of the rightness of BEING, what you have is usually enough to give you what you truly need. You won't get what you want, but you will get what you need. And this is why almost everybody who's got long-term sobriety and serenity in AA is prosperous no matter what level of income they're at. They aren't all driving Cadillacs, but they have what they need, and then some.

Now in my case I obviously needed an awful lot because my higher power has showered me with the most outrageous abundance I've ever seen. In fact, one time recently I was saying to my higher power, "Hey, how come you've given me all this, because I've got royalties rolling in and all kinds of other stuff. At times I've got checks lying around I haven't even cashed yet. And the higher power said, "That's because it takes a lot of money to calm down a nervous guy like you." Now a higher power isn't supposed to talk that way, but that's what mine had to say to me.

So I said, "Okay, man, if that's the way you feel, well I'll just kind of lean back and try to make the best of it and not have these guilt complexes about it. And I'll handle the money as well as I can. And when I'm halfway calmed down, if somebody comes and takes something away from me I won't argue too much." And the higher power says back, "I know that."

I can see now that in my advertising days I was going at life backward. I wanted HAVING a $75,000 income. So I would DO what I had to do to HAVE that income. Then I had to BE an advertising man so I could DO advertising and HAVE that big income.

When I finally accepted myself as I was, I can see now I went in search of my essential BEING. And I would accept any of the DOING and HAVING that came out of that BEING. So I followed my nose into teaching and went to Montana and lived in a little house and gave up all my previous desires to have fame and money. What is so humorous is that once I gave up the pursuit of those things I got them. But that really isn't the point; in fact, it obscures the point. Many people now say, "I'd accept life like you did, Jess, if I knew I'd get what you got." But that wasn't what I did. I didn't accept life to accomplish certain external ends. I went in search of my essential BEING so I could find some peace. And I got a measure of peace. And I was pretty happy with life *before* I got the abundance I now have. I couldn't have written my first book without a measure of peace and calm in my life. And I wrote it despite a full-time job and a serious illness, not out of a great discipline, but I did it fairly easily and naturally, without much effort. Acceptance works. But not for a person who says, "I'll accept myself as I am so I know I'll get to have all the things you have." That's not acceptance. That's a horse trade.

I think the reason self-acceptance works is that there is a harmony out there, there is a lawfulness. I was telling a lady about the trout stream of life one time. I said I realized I had to get out of the current and stop fighting the river. No sooner had I realized that than I saw there was a rock right by me. So I swam over to the quiet water behind the rock and the current eddied around and brought me all the food I needed. I just had to reach up for it. I could live just with a fraction of the effort I had used before. My mind and myself were free for all kinds of lovely things. She said, "What do you call your rock? Is it security rock or safety rock, or what?"

"No," I said. "It's harmony rock. The rock and I live in harmony. Its purpose is to serve me and my purpose is to take advantage of what it offers to me." To me acceptance is the beginning of harmony. And self-acceptance, in my experience, is where we start.

THREE

How We Run Away from Our Inner Self

Self-acceptance leads us deeper and deeper into ourselves to a beautiful guidance system we all can use: the still, quiet voice of the spirit. The word "spirit" is a fancy name for the feeling inside us that tells us what's right for us and what we believe in. It seems to me there are two predominant voices inside us that speak to us. One is the voice of the self-centered self, which is concerned with controlling the world outside us, controlling what people will think of us, and controlling events around us so we get what we want. There is another voice which tells us what is really right for us. It is the voice that prompted one of the Jews in the concentration camp that Viktor Frankl tells of to divide up his day's ration of bread and give it to the six sickest men in the hut. It is the voice Roberto Assagioli in *Psychosynthesis* calls the Higher Self as opposed to the conscious self. It is the voice the

Christians call Holy Spirit. It is the voice the other great religions speak of under various names. But it is also the voice that is so deadened by living completely in the self-centered self that most people say, "I still don't know what it is."

It's like I had two radios in my house. One radio, the voice of the spirit, had been turned down low for so long that the volume knob had rusted solid. So, once I decided I wanted to listen to that radio, instead of the noisy one, I had to go and sit real close to it and put my finger in the ear facing the noisy radio to drown it out. Then, as my senses got better tuned to the weak sound, I was able to hear it much more clearly.

Another problem is that we just don't talk of spiritual things much in our society. And because they have been so much neglected and so long neglected, we have, as Laurens Van der Post says, "lost the whole natural language of the spirit." That's why I can talk about the spirit with almost complete understanding to an American Indian, a Quaker, or a Pentecostal but not to most of my neighbors. I can get up twenty conversations on money with the first twenty people I meet. But I have to go a long way to get up a conversation on things spiritual. Yet I believe all of us are making our own spiritual quest. As I see a spiritual quest, it is seeking the uniqueness of our own being so we can get in harmony with the higher power and be the self we were meant to be. I think each of us is making our own spiritual quest the best way we know. But look how handicapped we are in our spiritual quest when we don't have words to talk with and hardly anyone to talk to.

Spirit is something that is especially hard to talk about in psychology because so much of psychology is so opposed to spirit or inner voice. And spirit is hard to talk about with a great many other people because they confuse spirit or inner voice with a religion that has failed them and that they fear or dislike.

Even worse, spirit and inner voice seem to be opposed to the mind and what we think of as rational thoughts. The power to think and figure things out—one of the things we've so commonly thought is so great about Western civilization—is its biggest mess, the saddest thing. In the last three hundred to four hundred years we built up the mind as all powerful, threw out the spirit part of us along with the God business, and said, "We will do it all with our heads, we're so smart."

This applies to psychology, my science, particularly. Tearing itself away from philosophy, like an angry little child leaving home, it said, "Father philosophy, you're crazy. We in psychology don't want to have any part of you, we don't want to have any more to do with you. So we will throw out all philosophy. All philosophy is dead and we're breaking all ties with you. It's all dead and valueless." We threw out the wash water but the baby went with it.

To my mind, the thing we've got to do is retrieve the baby. It's not a matter of breathing some life back into that baby, because it never dies to us. We may die to it, but it never dies to us. You may feel that this doesn't apply to you because you don't believe in God. But everybody's got a god. What you bow your knee down to, what you put first in your life, what has the highest priority in your life, that's what your god is. Our god can be anger, our god can be hate. I used to think that a god was just something you worshiped. All the god did was punish or reward you at the end of your life. I didn't see that a god had a power that was of any immediate help to me. But that's really what we are looking for when we make a god out of money or social position or sex. We're looking for something that gives us power to control some things. But there is so much left that we can't control. And that's why we need some power outside ourselves, some higher power. If I can look in the mirror and believe the person I'm looking at is all the power there is, then I'm really in tough shape.

So we who are so smart, we of this advanced Western civilization who have made so much material progress, we open-minded scientists, we have erected a new god, our mind, to take the place of the one we threw out. To me it looks like our new god doesn't work very well.

As I say, it's not a question of if I'm going to have a god or a higher power in my life, it's just a question of what it's going to be. Most of us have made a god of ourselves. I worshiped the god of the mind, but that's just another variation of self. So is the god of money. Our worship and belief in them let our life break down. When we have ourselves at the center, our life breaks down at the center. That's what gives us those bad nights, the dark nights of the soul. And not all dark nights of the soul are at nighttime after we go to bed and then wake up in the middle of the night when things look so terrible. Some of them are in the daytime when the world turns to ashes in our mouths.

When that happens, I see it as a useful experience. Just as a thermometer is valuable to tell us how warm to dress when we go out on a cold day, so are those dark nights of the soul useful ways of telling us how the state of our relationship to our higher power is. The stronger and deeper the sense of our higher power, the less problems I see we have in life. In my experience it isn't a matter of finding a higher power that's theologically correct. I'm looking at a higher power in terms of how that belief can change my life. And I'm looking for the most powerful higher power I can find. I have no power of my own to speak of. I'm powerless in the important things in my life. I can change a tire but I can't change my personality. So the more power my higher power's got, then the better shape I'm in.

I've come to see it's purely a matter of utility. What kind of higher power can do the absolute most for me in my life? And who can I learn from who's got the kind of higher power that's doing a lot for them? And I look to see if there is some way my concept of a higher power is faulty in relation to theirs because theirs is doing more for them than mine is doing for me. So I'm not looking at theological correctness. I'm looking at utility because I've seen the need for this concept in my life. I've lived without it for a long time. I lived both with no belief in a higher power and I lived with a so-called religious belief in a higher power that was purely a dead religion. It was just mouth music.

I see a lot of religious folks who come to me and say, "Jess, I'm having this or that kind of problem." And what the problem shows is a complete lack of faith in themselves, in their fellow men and women or the world at large and the higher power who's running the whole thing. I want to say, "Hey, you're claiming to have some religion. Faith is supposedly the product of your religion yet you don't show me any more faith than you can put on the head of a pin." They kind of shake their heals and they don't seem to grasp what I'm talking about. But typically they've got a dead religion.

They've come by their religion formally. I've come to my belief in a higher power in a different way, purely from the point of utility. I didn't care where I looked as long as I could find a higher power that could do something. Now that I've come to this point a lot of theologians are saying, "Hey, Jess, you're right theologically." Now that's interesting but that isn't what I tried to be. I even thought when I started out on this search that I was leaving all theology behind and just looking for what was right for me. I was looking for that still quiet voice inside me. So that's where I started and those were the lines I pursued.

A lady wrote "Dear Abby." She said, "Abby, I have been on a big campaign to stop people from overusing the word 'wise' as in 'time-wise.' But I'm tempted to give up that crusade for another one. Now I want to stop people from using the expression 'making love' when what they really mean is 'having sex.'" So this poor lady is considering going to work on that problem instead. To me that is a beautiful example of the grandiosity that's in us. No small problems for me like who's going to change the tires on the car today, I'm going to change the whole American language. And I wonder if it possibly occurred to her there in Massillon, Ohio, or Podunk, Iowa, that she's thinking of going out singlehandedly and minding everybody else's business and thereby change the whole world. I thought that letter was a good example of the way many of us really feel and I know it's the way I used to feel. Talk about grandiosity.

Like I said, I wanted to decide if it was going to rain, I wanted to be sure and remind God to bring the sun up tomorrow morning, He might forget. I didn't want anything to go on without my approval. When you're that busy, you don't have any time for vacations. And that is a complete lack of faith. It was in this context that I quoted my old friend Vince, who said, "If I want to live the abundant life I've got to stop fighting for complete control.

If you want to live abundantly, you must surrender. There ain't no money nor job nor power that can help you get rid of grief. You've got to accept God or be God." That is the simplest I've ever heard the matter put. You've got to accept some higher power, some power outside yourself or you've got to be it. When you try being God, you're all the power there is.

When I finally had the matter put to me as bluntly as Vince did, I could see that I had better get out of the God business. I wasn't suited for it. And then, when I saw the limits of my life, I saw that I had a choice between any kind of god I wanted. I could have a very limited god or I could have a god who had all power. I thought when you've got a choice like that it's simple. You take the highest power god you can find. Then I found the limitation of power was not a matter of limitation of the higher power but my making contact with that power and turning things over to it. Any limitations I have experienced in my relations to my higher power has been due only to my limited capacity to let go, to trust to my higher power.

I've been rewarded so abundantly for what little I've turned over to my higher power, you'd think, "Any fool, Jess, would give up a lot more—instantly." If you gave seventy-five cents to a guy and he gave you ten farms in return, you'd think you'd be smart enough to give him a couple of dollars. But not me. I give up slow. I come in hard. But that's okay. I'm a slow learner but I tend to hang on to my lesson pretty well. That's the advantage I have as a teacher. I'm a real dramatic example for you so you can look at me and say, "Boy, I don't need to do all the things as dumb as he did them. I can short cut some of those mud holes he got himself bogged down in." Because if every one of us had to make every mistake then there would be no point, you see, in us talking with each other because it would mean each of us has to make every mistake and there's no point in learning from others. Fortunately, we can learn from others' mistakes.

In many ways I am stupid and hard-to-teach. But there's one way I'm very discriminating and perceptive. I seek out good teaching. I look at people who are very good at living life. I ask them questions. When they answer, I listen. When my teachers talk, I never argue. When I pick out a person to teach me something, I do absolutely nothing but listen very quietly, very patiently, and with much respect.

Many times I don't understand all my teachers say but even then I'm inclined not to question. I have found that if I don't understand usually it's a sign I'm not ready to learn yet. I'll just keep coming back and coming back and I'll get what I can and eventually I will understand more.

I learned some respect for the value of the right teacher for me from the Zen tradition where students go from one Zen school to another until they find the man who really speaks to them. They go up to the man, the Zen teacher, and say, "You are my teacher." And the Zen teacher says, "Good." And the student stays there and studies with him.

Many people had written me wanting to come here to Bozeman in the summer and have me be their teacher. I ignored those letters for years before I realized my mistake. Now I have a special school of my own here each year in the last week in July, where any of my readers can come. I finally saw that it was as wrong for the teacher to deny the student as it was for the student to refuse to recognize his teacher.

Now in our dumb, so-called modern way we have very little respect for that kind of tradition. Like pigs going to slaughter, we take our teachers as they come to us. I'm horrified at this in the students of the university. I used to ask the students in my classes at the beginning of the quarter, "How many of you know anything about what you're getting in for in my class?" There were three or four of us teachers handling the many sections of the same Educational Psychology class each quarter. Most of the students didn't have any idea what they were getting in for. They didn't even take the trouble to ask some of their fellow students, "Hey, what's Lair like?"

Which students take the trouble to find out what they're getting in for? They're not the A students, they're the C students: the jocks and the hippies and the sorority sex pots. They are the ones who are more discriminating about who they put themselves in contact with than the so-called brains, the intellects.

Many of our A students are the dumbest people I've ever seen. One of my students once said, "Jess, isn't there something good you can say about a four-point grade average [straight A]?" "I can't think of what it would be," I said. He was so put down. I said, "If you've got a four-point average in some quarters at school it would be all right, but to get straight A's every quarter you've got to lay down and play dead." We university instructors are so capricious in our grading that we can't be that clear and consistent at identifying a talent, no matter how bright you are. We demand that you think just like we want you to and if you don't we won't give you an A. The way to get A's in college classes consistently is by knowing what the teacher wants and lying on the tests. That means you either have to cave in to the teacher and lay down and play dead a little bit or you just cold-bloodedly lie to the guy about what you think, knowing you're finessing him.

But that's what we've exalted in our civilization, the intellect. How a puny thing like that can be so exalted is hard to understand except for our need for certainty. We need assurance that we're following all the rules. It's the old legalism of following the letter of the law instead of the spirit, risen up in a new form. Science appeals to us because it seems so exact. But even physics is exact only to a small mind. The theoretical physicists know how inexact physics really is.

I remember reading the Old Testament stories. The Jews would have a couple of hundred years of good times and then they would have a hundred years of raising hell and catching misery and I thought what a stupid people. Here we're doing the same thing again, just in a different form. I can see now why it happens. You no sooner catch hell from life for one vice and get that halfway stamped out in your system and think you've got it made when a new devil comes in the back window disguised as a lamb and you think, "Welcome, brother." He turns out to be a wolf in sheep's clothing and you're half devoured before you even know what's up.

So I've learned a lot of things as I've looked at this higher power problem more carefully. Many of the questions I had as a kid cleared up. A lot of people want to tell me about their faith and simultaneously want to talk about their fear and anxiety. Fear and anxiety can come in only when faith is gone or temporarily absent.

But they say, "Oh no. That's not true. I'm a very religious person. I've got a lot of faith."

I say, "Well, please demonstrate some for me in this predicament."

"Well," they say, "you're so wrong. I do have faith but I'm frightened."

It's like Abdullah says, "When we worry, we insult God."

I used to think faith was something you prayed for. It

may be but I haven't found any that way. The way I got what little faith I have is illustrated by a story told by Father Martin.

A guy fell over the edge of a cliff but as he fell he was able to catch hold of a tree. He hollered, "Hey, can somebody up there help me?"

A deep voice answered, "This is God. I want you to follow my instructions. First, let go of the tree."

At this the guy's fear of letting go was too strong and he yelled, "Is there anybody else up there?"

That story was me. And there was no one else up there. I didn't let go of the tree. My hands finally gave out and so the matter of letting go was taken out of my own hands. But when I fell, I found I only dropped a foot. There was a ledge under me I hadn't been able to see. Since then I've been more and more able to let go of the tree and there's always a good support for me. Finally, I'm getting some faith. As you can see, for me, faith didn't come in answer to prayer, it came as a result of a practical demonstration I was given over and over again.

A lot of people want to talk about the evil in the world and who do you think is the first bad thing they light on? They light on Hitler. You know what the real bad thing in the world is? One bad thing is the terrible thing we did to our friend—today. And the other bad thing was making ourselves God. And any person who has to go back in history fifty years to what Hitler did to find a bad thing is crazy. I grant that what Hitler did was a monstrous thing. It's a good illustration of how dead religion can be when Luther's country, a supposedly Christian country, does the most monstrous act that's ever been committed on the face of this earth. To me that's a good demonstration of dead religion carried to its absolute, complete, asinine extreme. Sure Hitler led the killing of the Jews. But he and his regime needed the support of the good churchgoing Germans to do what he did.

What happened there should be a beautiful lesson to anybody who wants to stick to a legalistic view of their religion. "Boy, ain't I got religion. I've got my church. You just ask my minister." I hear a lot of people who say that. I want to call them on it but if I do I fall in their trap and I don't want to be in that trap. One of the bad twists we give religion is piety where we say the proper prayers at all the proper times. And one of the most extreme examples is one Bob Mumford talks about, which is the man sitting in his room watching Billy Graham on television with the door locked so none of God's nosey children can come in there and disturb his beautiful religious feeling. That's narcissism. It's thinking religion consists of Jesus and me on the mountaintop.

What I've come to see is that it is very hard for us to know for sure what's right or wrong. There is simply following the spirit, following our own conscience as well as we can follow it. I'm not in the judgment business. That's my higher power's business to decide whether I did right or wrong. This is pretty hard to explain. I know it might be difficult for some of you. I'm trying to communicate to you what I feel, what I've found, and some of this stuff I've found, I may change my mind on at a moment's notice. But as near as I can see now, I can't see what's right or wrong very clearly. I can simply know what's best for me at this moment.

All I've got control of is what I'm going to say and do in the next five minutes. And I don't know whether what I'm going to say is right or wrong. I'm just going to say the best thing that I can say with my attention as solidly on that time as it possibly can be, without being distracted too much by the past or the future.

I know that right now I've got some things swimming in the back of my head I don't know about, and that's a lot different than it used to be when I could only talk to you with about half of my mind because in the other half of my mind all my troubles and preoccupations were working back there.

I've seen that there are two kinds of doing. There's doing and there's not doing. Not doing is a kind of doing. This is the old thing you've heard about as sins of omission—the sins you commit by not doing anything. If I stand and watch a kid in the street and a car's coming, I've got to try to get him out of the street. If I don't try to get him out of the street, that's not the best thing to do at that moment.

I decide at any moment what I should be doing or what I should be not doing. One of the big things I should be not doing, and I've tried to resist it as much as I can during my time with you, I should be not doing things that mess in your life. I should be staying away from your spiritual quest. Each of you have your own way to find in life. I should not be interfering in that.

As I said earlier, when I condemn myself I condemn an innocent man because in the past five minutes I was doing the best I could. It used to be that my mind was so full with what was right that I couldn't see what was good. So now I try to look for the good.

I have found that one of the rarest ways of handling a problem that I see around is giving it the spiritual treatment, which is bringing meditation, bringing whatever wisdom you can command from your higher power to bear on the problem. A lot of times it means waiting on the problem. But we want to give all the problems the rational treatment. We want to make a list on two sides of the paper for and against. And we cross out a "for" that balances with an "against." And we see which side ends up with the most "fors" or "againsts" and we go ahead and do that. That's the stupid way to solve a problem.

Most rational treatments are about as irrational as anything I've ever seen. But they give us a nice comfortable feeling of, "I'm a scientist and I'm a modern day man and I'm using my great mind." And many people see religious beliefs as offering them a nice, fine set of ways to be perfect. That's a terrible distortion which comes out of our own need and fear, fear of doing things, fear of taking a chance, the fear of being imperfect. So we think it's supposed to be that way. As I see religion it was originally built to heal sick people like me. It was made to help the downtrodden and the sinners of the world rather than the righteous. In fact, as near as I can read those religions, they warn against self-righteousness, they warn against assuming the virtues.

In the twelve-step programs like Alcoholics Anonymous and Emotions Anonymous the members of those programs assume the absence of the virtues. They come to the meetings admitting the complete absence of the virtues. They say, "Hey, I'm a worthless, rotten, no good neurotic, or alcoholic or addict or overeater or gambler." And the more gravy spots you've got on your tie, the better. If you've got shoes that don't match and pants out of the Salvation army bin, beautiful, come right in and have a cup of coffee. That brotherhood takes in people that the people in churches can't stand and that even their own mothers can't love any more.

A lot of people say, "Well, it's going too far to say any of us are completely absent of the virtues." I really don't see that it is. Most of us, it seems to me, are so far from virtue that to quibble whether we are completely absent of virtue or almost completely absent of virtue is kind of silly.

I've been inspired by what I see happen to people who are in twelve-step fellowships. I've come to see and have a great, great faith in a higher power that takes care of things. That way I can have some vacations. There's a great freedom that comes when I don't have to be my own god. A lot of people want to say, "Boy, if I'm not worrying about something, who's going to worry about it?" I say, "Well, what are you going to do about it?" "Nothing," they say. "But boy, am I doing a beautiful job of being concerned with the problem and worrying about it. And who's going to be concerned about it and worry about it if I don't? And what will get done about that problem if a great, caring person like me doesn't worry about it?"

You can carry out that line of thinking to its extreme and really bring out how ridiculous it really is. In this matter I've got the edge on many of you because I'm so well aware of the foolishness and egotism behind what pretends to be concern because I've spent so much time doing that myself.

I've talked about a couple of the different ways we try to run away from the truth that is inside us. I've talked about how we try to run our lives completely on reason and why that breaks down. And I've talked about how we take religion and kill the vitality in it by turning it into law and legalism instead of following the spirit.

It isn't that there is anything wrong with learning and rational thought. They are great in their place. And there's nothing wrong with religion. It's great, too, but when religion is distorted too far, it stops being of any value to the person who distorts it.

There's another distortion that's gone on and that is in

psychology. One of the basic questions facing us is the degree of freedom we have over our actions.

The two simultaneous main currents of psychology which have had a drastic influence on the thinking of Western European civilization are those fostered by Pavlov and Freud. Pavlov and his conditioning and Freud's emphasis on early childhood can be used to support an idea that our behavior is almost completely determined. In a new form we have the old religious determination. And this new religion is particularly American because no other country in the world has distorted these two men's ideas to the extreme that we have. I think we need to look more closely at the implications of Pavlov's and Freud's work. Everything in your training goes directly against what I'm going to say so please bear with me.

As I mentioned earlier, we are in the top wheelhouse running this ship and there is another guy in that lower wheelhouse who's got the button where he can take over control and steer our rudder. The upper set of controls doesn't work any more. The little guy in the subconscious has taken over and he's running the ship up on a sandbar because that's where he wants to go.

It's obvious that the conscious mind doesn't control. What's our answer to this? Freud gave us one answer and Pavlov gave us another. They were right as far as they went. But I think the evidence is piling up that neither Freud's ideas nor Pavlov's could carry the weight that's been put on them.

Freud told us that the subconscious mind controlled; it was distorted and warped by our childhood experiences and had all those hidden desires, basically stemming out of sexual difficulties. The subconscious mind controlled and we better do what it wanted to do, it was bad to repress it. That wasn't just the way those ideas were presented, but that's not too far from the way they were received. One corruption of Freud's ideas is that you should let the spoiled kid tear down the house, you can always replace it. You shouldn't repress him.

Pavlov showed us how the dog would salivate when Pavlov rang the bell for food (and I started salivating as I finished writing that sentence). When you show a dog some food in a dish and ring the bell, pretty soon you can just ring the bell and the dog will salivate. But the dog stops salivating after a while unless food is again presented with the bell. Without presenting food, that salivation response that was conditioned extinguishes, it dies out.

Okay, so people say, I'm conditioned, I'm programmed. I've got these tapes running in my head. (I don't mean this to knock transactional analysis but this is just representative of the kind of things you hear.) But there's a small fly in that ointment, my friends. The only thing you can condition is an unconditioned reflex like salivation that we have little or no conscious control over. But there are a very limited number of unconditioned reflexes to be conditioned—the salivation reflex, the eye blink, the knee jerk. And even worse, any response that is conditioned extinguishes or dies out if it isn't maintained by reconditioning. So there's no such thing as conditioning someone and then they stay conditioned the rest of their lives.

The excuse "I was conditioned" is used so widely without regard for the fact there has to be a reflex to hook up the conditioning to. Now you can make some tenuous links. A classic one is the case of Goebbels' propaganda in Germany. We say Goebbels conditioned the Germans to hate the Jews. That's a bunch of crap. What Goebbels did was to tell the German people, "The scapegoat for your misery is the Jews." Why did it work? Very simple. The Germans had a fairly long history of prejudice against the Jews and they wanted to believe it. You can't condition anybody when you aren't using an unconditioned reflex like the knee jerk or salivation. So you can't condition people-unless they want to believe it. I can prove that to you very simply. Imagine Goebbels trying to tell the German people, "You're just looking for an out. You want a scapegoat. You yourself are the source of all your troubles here in the 1930s. You fools haven't been able to run a country yet for any period of time. And you need a big father or you can't operate." You try selling that to the German people and they would kill you in a week.

Okay, if to condition someone, they have to want what you're going to condition them to, who's conditioning who? You've got no control over them through conditioning. You're a creature of them. It's like the two rats who were talking to each other. One rat said, "I've got this psychologist completely under my control. Every time I press the bar, he gives me a food pellet." Goebbels had to tell the Germans what they wanted to hear. What they wanted to hear was obvious. They were already feeling what Goebbels told them. All he did was agree with what they were previously feeling.

The problem we have comes from the use of the word conditioning. In psychology we use the word conditioning for two different processes: classical conditioning and operant conditioning. The two kinds of conditioning are as different as night and day. Even psychologists don't always keep the two kinds of conditioning well separated.

Classical conditioning is Pavlov's kind of conditioning, where you control the subject by working on a reflex that is already tightly linked to the response you want. If you want someone to salivate, you show them food. If you want their knee to jerk, you hit their tendon with a rubber hammer. You can even brainwash someone by locking them up and turning their world upside down.

But for classical conditioning to work you have to have a reflex to work with and there are only a few. Or, you have to have control of people by locking them up or having them as your children where you can control them for a while.

One other problem of classical conditioning is that it wears off. Once you are out of a prison or a bad childhood setting, you don't need to keep acting the same way. If it weren't for this fact, bad early childhood environments would produce all criminals. But we know that doesn't happen and most people break free.

So when we look at classical conditioning as a reason for our problems, there are a lot of loopholes in our argument.

The other kind of conditioning is operant conditoning. This is really exactly opposite classical conditioning yet it has the same basic word involved. Operant conditioning could more sensibly be called reward learning. It is the learning of behavior through rewarding that behavior.

I think psychologists have pretty well agreed that at least 90 per cent of our behavior is learned through the rewards we receive. What is such a crucial difference between reward learning and classical conditioning is that in reward learning the person doing the learning is substantially in control. If I do respond it's because I do like the reward whether I will admit it or not.

Much of our early environment, especially outside the home where we had more freedom, was reward learning. We did what we did because we liked the rewards we got.

So the problem with the word "conditioned" is that

most of the time we use it, we are referring to reward learning and to things we did for those rewards. But "conditioned" carries the old Pavlovian implication that we were forced to do something and in most cases we weren't forced. And even in those cases where we may have been forced at one time we aren't being forced any more.

They say we advertising people condition minds. We can't sell you anything you don't want to buy. If the product doesn't reward you, you won't buy it. That's why, despite powerful advertising, most new products fail. If you don't want a product, no amount of advertising can sell it to you. Movies are a good example. Some low budget, low advertised movies have swept the country. Expensive turkeys like *Cleopatra* bombed and millions in advertising and publicity couldn't make people go see that movie. Also, I've seen lots of cases in advertising of products that were overnight successes but died soon because they had no lasting value.

Using conditioning as the basis for our argument, we can say, "Poor me. I'm conditioned. Because of my lousy background who can expect anything out of me?" There is increasing evidence that the chance you will commit a crime has more relation to the chance you will be punished than any other statistic. Now, if a crime is a product of environment, solely, then crime rates should not react to the certainty of punishment.

There is a strong current of psychology and sociology in America that's grown up of "poor baby, you couldn't help what you did. With your parents, and your environment, who could help it?" The only hole in that philosophy is, you get ten kids coming out of a family and typically eight or nine of them do a nice job with their lives and one is a criminal. Well, how come, if the environment is the whole explanation for the one criminal, how come the nine didn't go the same way?

And this is the big thing that to me is giving us more grief right now than most any other problem I've seen and that is this one of "poor baby, you couldn't help it. You're overdetermined. Your behavior is all determined for you."

The most beautiful example I see is, again, in the people of AA. These guys do not come out of Sunday schools. Some of them come off skid rows where, when they are acting up, they take the minimum of three to four policemen apiece to handle them. A high percentage of a police force's time is used to handle the alcohol and drug problem. If their behavior was so determined, how come, on some given day these alcoholics changed from night to day? And then all of a sudden, five years later, they're driving a Cadillac, their Cadillac that they own. And they aren't running a string of gals to support it.

I frankly do not buy the conditioning argument or the Freudian argument of our parents screwing up. Where does that leave all people who didn't have bad parents? I've never seen a set of parents who could raise a kid so bad that you could guarantee that he would be no good. I've seen the worst kind of folks come out of both very good homes and very bad ones.

Now I grant you that in the nature of the crime there's some correlation. Some of those folks who come out of very good homes might be much more inclined to what we call white collar crime and some of the folks out of bad homes are inclined to be in dumb crimes like knocking over a grocery store. That's very messy, you could get killed by the grocer. And you could get sent up for ten years for stealing eighty dollars when you can steal $100,-000 in white collar crime and get a couple of years. But

I'm lumping both kinds of crime together. I figure they're both crime.

I see people as having a great deal of control over what they do. We do have a choice. As I told you this could be very hard for you because it goes against everything you feel you know. A whole, big part of our society is based on the fact of "Poor baby, you couldn't help it. So we will rehabilitate you and try to make up for the bad things that have been done to you."

This point of view includes the proposition that we can't lead good lives until we wipe out poverty, sickness, and crime. That's not a spiritual belief, that's the rankest kind of materialism and it ignores the point that spiritual poverty is a cause of poverty, crime, and sickness rather than being caused by them. It's easy to demonstrate that in the case of the very well off people in this country which is at least half of us. I don't see that we are a bit more spiritual just because we aren't hungry and we have a secure income. And I've seen spiritual poverty among the very rich that is just as bad as anything I've seen among the very poor people. At this the materialists shout, "But he's got money to ease the pain." The answer is that must not help much or why would the pain be so bad that suicide is common. One high risk suicide group is the prostitutes. But right up there with them are dentists and psychiatrists.

"But," say the materialists, "how can you be spiritual when you're hungry?" In India and Asia we see that most of the spiritual teachers, and monks live in poverty, eating only when somebody gives them food.

So I think, in applying Pavlov and Freud as the gods of our social problems, we have shifted too much of the responsibility away from the individual and onto his past and his environment. I've never seen a past or an environment so bad an individual couldn't to some degree overcome it. I've never see an environment or a past so good that an individual couldn't throw it away.

There is an altogether different psychological view which I think works. I believe in the basic psychology I mentioned earlier that we do things for the rewards that they give us. And when what we do stops being rewarding to us, we stop doing it. The only flaw in that and the reason it's very unpleasant psychology is it makes us look at our actions and their consequences. You and I have to look at what we've done and say, "My God, you mean to say I really want the results of this sick game."

Here's a true example. The wife of an alcoholic got beat on so she ended up in a hospital and then divorced the alcoholic. She married another guy, he beat on her, she ended up in a hospital. She divorced him and married another guy. He beat on her and she ended up in the hospital. It was a small town so the doctor knew her well. He asked her, "Honey, doesn't this strike you as some kind of a pattern?" She said, "What do you mean?"

Now the doctor's point is very clear to us in that extreme case partly because we're outside the problem and can see it more clearly than when we're the one getting beat on. But I find, unfortunately, those same sad, repetitive experiences in my own life. And I find that once those sick rewards stop being important to me I finally get ready to give up that sick game. Like I said, I haven't been used in the last three years. Isn't it funny that the world all of a sudden decided to stop using people?

He who lives by the sword must die by the sword. I've got to take my lumps. I've got to say that most of the sad and bad and troublesome things that happen to me in life I bring about. In some cases we don't bring it about. Like I said about the woman who has to marry a man she can look down on, an emotional cripple; she didn't specifically want to marry an alcoholic, she didn't want to get beat in. But a part of her did want and need to marry someone she could look down on. Those other things are just consequences of the original choice to meet a sick need.

We like to say, "The devil made me do it." There is a great line from Tagore, the Indian poet. "Who was it, prisoner, who forged those chains of yours so carefully? 'It was I,' said the prisoner, 'who forged these chains so carefully.'"

You see, if someone else laid this problem on me then only someone else can take it off me but the hope is, if I laid this problem on myself then I can take it off. Look at your life today and your past and see if you don't honestly have more freedom of action than you thought at first. See, too, if you're willing to admit that that magnificent intellect of yours just can't solve all your problems. And see if maybe your opposition to the deadness you see in religion isn't coming more from people and institutions than it is from ideas. Because only if you're willing and able to put aside ghosts and dead issues can you openly look at the source that I see directs everyone's life to one degree or another—the clear sweet voice of the spirit that lies deep within us waiting to be listened to.

FOUR

The Deepest Self:
Finding and Following Our Inner Voice

I know a number of people in Alcoholics Anonymous. So even though I'm not an alcoholic, I've had a chance to see deeply into that program. I now see there is a powerful lesson for psychology and theology in AA and the other twelve-step programs like Emotions Anonymous, Gamblers Anonymous, Parents Anonymous (for child abuse), and other "anonymous" organizations.[1]

[1] For information on twelve-step programs, write:

EA.   Emotions Anonymous, P.O. Box 4245,
      St. Paul, Minnesota 55104
AA.   Alcoholics Anonymous, P.O. Box 459
      Grand Central Station, New York, N.Y. 10017
OA.   Overeaters Anonymous, 3730 Motor Avenue,
      Los Angeles, California 90034
PA.   Parents Anonymous (for child abuse) 250 West 57th
      Street, New York, N.Y. 10019
GA.   Gamblers Anonymous, P.O. Box 59415,
      North Iowa Station, Chicago, Illinois 60659

There are also groups of people with emotional problems using the twelve-steps calling themselves NA, Neurotics Anonymous, and EHA, Emotional Health Anonymous. Look in your phone directory under EA, NA, or EHA or classified ads. Or write EA for help.

I've begun to see that there are some universal principles that operate in life that govern the emotions and the subconscious. More and more I've come to feel that deep inside yourself and myself is where we need to go to find what truly works in life.

There's a song called "Where Shall We Hide the Truth?"[2] All the first parts of the song are about where we couldn't hide the truth from man. We could hide it on the mountaintop and he would go there and find it. We could hide it in the ocean but he would dive down and get it. We could hide it in the atom and his curiosity would take him there. "Where shall we hide the truth from man?" And the writer comes up finally with the answer and this answer just chills your spine.

You know what the answer is, don't you? "Hide it in his soul, he'll live without it. Even if we reveal it and shout it, he won't believe the truth is in him." I don't mean "him" as "God Him," I mean him, you him, him and her. "Hide it in his heart, he will doubt it, hide it in his soul, he'll live without it."

How can it be? What a stupid place to put the truth. Inside of me? It can't be. Yet I have given the most powerful demonstration a person could ever have of the truth being in me.

When I had my heart attack, I said I'm never again going to do anything I don't believe in. I had, at that time, the advantage of four religions. I had been raised a Baptist on my own volition, not out of force. I was baptized a Baptist when I was twelve. I switched to being a Methodist in Minneapolis not out of force but because they loved me enough to let me play basketball on their team. Then

2 The Universe Is Singing—*Songs in the Spirit of Teilhard de Chardin,* words, music by Sebastian Temple (Ephram Publications, G.I.A. records, 7404 S. Mason Ave., Chicago, Ill. 60638.).

I became a Unitarian. Actually I have five religions, because after being a Unitarian, then I was nothing. Ten years before my heart attack, I became a Catholic and went to Mass every day.

I really worked hard at those religions. I gave them a good run for their money. I even questioned some of those preachers. "There is something that I can't find here. Can you tell me how I can find the answers to some of these questions I have?" One preacher said, "Go and look in Butler's book." Well I had read enough books by then to know that the chances were that one more wouldn't make much difference. And I'm sure the answer wasn't there.

So when I had my heart attack I did what I thought at the time was the most selfish thing in the world. I finally said, "Never again am I going to do anything I don't believe in." I wasn't going in search of what the Baptists, the Methodists, the Unitarians, the agnostics, or the Catholic Church believed in. "I'm going in search of what I believe in. I'm not going ever again to do anything I don't believe in." So I pursued that line quite a while.

I sent a copy of my first book to Father Moorman, the priest we had back in St. Paul, a wonderful man. He wrote me the strangest letter. He said, "Jess, I've preached a number of sermons out of your book. Your book is a wonderful manual for spiritual development."

I thought, "The poor man is crazy." I'm not spiritual. I'm not religious. I did a very selfish thing. I went to find out what I believed in. I went within. And the only thing in life that I think I could guarantee 100 per cent is that any of you who goes and looks for the truth will find it. Seek and ye shall find. You won't find perfect, complete truth immediately, but if you look for truth honestly and diligently, you'll be rewarded.

93

We just go deep within, and listen to that voice that's inside each of us. It's not that self-centered voice that tells us what to do or what not to do to make people think well of us. It's that higher-power centered voice that tells us what is for our own deepest and best interests. I know that voice has got to be in folks like you. I deal with people off skid row and I know those seeming derelicts, the ones who will come up to you in the late afternoon and breathe on you with that foul breath for a handout, they have that deep, quiet voice within. Those folks have a voice inside of them that's just as dependable as the one I found inside of me and the one inside of anyone else that seeks for guidance. So there's the guide to our search for truth. That's what we have been given to rely on.

To me, listening to our inner voice means listening as hard as we can to that little voice inside that speaks for the spirit. In my experience, all my problems come from following the voice of the self—the ego. To hear the little voice of the spirit, I've got to listen very, very carefully so the voice of the ego doesn't drown out the voice of the spirit. At first it's like trying to get a weather report from some faraway radio station. The local station is drowning that message. But if you listen very, very carefully, you can get enough of the words to find out the weather where you're going. Same with tuning in to that inner voice; the more you listen, the clearer it gets.

That spiritual voice puts us in harmony with ourselves, our higher power, and with life itself. When I talked of doing what was right for me, my students thought I was being selfish. I couldn't explain why this wasn't selfish, I just know it didn't work out that way. I see now why. When we listen to the voice of the self-centered self, the ego, that is selfish. And it is the kind of selfishness that really hurts us. It hurts our bodies, it confuses our minds and feelings, and we get out of harmony with the spirit. When we listen to that other voice inside, the voice of the spirit, we get a totally opposite effect. Because the spirit is in harmony with everything, listening to the voice of the spirit heals our body. It clears our mind and it develops our ability to hear the spirit voice better.

Since our spirit is in harmony with the higher power, just as everyone's spirit is, the minute we get in harmony with the spirit, we get in harmony with the spirits of everyone around us. So that's why getting in tune with our spirit voice isn't selfish, it's the exact opposite. It's the greatest thing we can do for anyone around us as well as ourselves.

The other person many not seem to be following his spirit very well as the time and, in that case, some of their actions may conflict with the people around them. But being in harmony with the spirit in them is enough to put us as much in harmony with them as we can be.

It's like each of us were vibrating musical notes. My violin string is vibrating at middle C, 256 vibrations per second in harmony with the highest power at 256 vibrations per second. Since everybody else's spirit is in harmony with the same higher power, then their spirit strings are vibrating at 256 per second. So that makes me in harmony with their spirit so when I follow the spirit that would be why it would work out so well for the people around me. Each of our instruments would be vibrating on the same note at the same time with the individual flavor our instrument gives the note. So if we were all in harmony, we would be like one huge, perfect symphony.

I see now that when I'm in a problem it's because I'm not accepting or I'm not doing what I can to change something I can change. So giving the problem the spiritual treatment means reflecting and meditating to see how I can get in harmony with life.

Often I will find myself in a problem where my own behavior or someone else's behavior is a problem for me. I will fall into self-pity: "How can I go on this way?" The answer to that question, I can see now, is simple. I won't have to go on this way. Nothing stays the same. The situation will change. It will get better, get worse, or go away. One of the biggest mistakes I make in that problem is not realizing how much I or the other person can be changed and how likely that is. At the time of my heart attack, I was going one way and then turned and started going another. My friend Vince was a hopeless alcoholic and nearly dead at forty-five. One Sunday afternoon in a park in Ogden, Utah, two AA's came up to him and told him failure was only in the grave. That was twenty-five years ago. But when we are in one of those situations, we can't see how we can get out of it. And often we can't, if we depend on our own power. But the higher power is always in there changing people when they finally are willing to give up and seek help.

Back in my religious days I was all confused about the truth. I thought it had to do with right or wrong. And I thought we could isolate truth from people and from actions. But I've seen now we can't. Truth does come out of principles. But principles aren't inflexible rules, they can only be guidelines.

For some time my teachers have been teaching me that truth is what works. If it doesn't work, it isn't truth. That's a startling idea because it turns the world upside down. If I'm trying to do right or wrong, I have to depend on the rules and other people to tell me that. But if I can learn truth by what works, then I am really the only person who can judge that question. It's just like in skiing.

I use basic principles Danny Morgan teaches me, and then I find how to get the best results from those principles in light of my special situation, my size and my weight, the snow, and my special physical limitations and strength. For example, my legs are strong and I have fair balance but I have lots of trouble keeping my right leg from making both turns. On a left turn it should do the work, but on a right turn it shouldn't or I'll fall. All my falls are on right turns. I find I can work on this problem by special drills and by paying attention. So I need to find out what works for me in skiing as well as life.

Another problem I had with the external authority saying, "right" or "wrong" was that it suggested if you didn't have an external authority there was no "right" or "wrong." Or it suggested you could change "right" or "wrong" by changing external authorities. If I wanted a divorce, I could switch from Catholic back to Methodist and it would change from "wrong" to "right."

I don't believe in that system of external authorities for me any more. I couldn't make it work. And I didn't see very many other people who could make it work for them.

We can't live just by a set of laws because there is no way you can write enough laws to cover every situation. So if you want to try to live strictly by law you'll find you're almost paralyzed because you can't find the exact law to cover your situation and they disagree completely. The way I see a lot of us handling this difficulty is we pick out a couple of laws and we really get fanatical about following them. We see we can't follow every law and that bothers us. So we go way overboard in following a few. The ones people pick out to follow most often are: I'm an honest person because I don't steal, and I'm a moral person because I don't jump in bed with the neighbor's wife. Both those statements are so full of holes that it is laughable. But there are people who run their lives centered on statements like that. Some minor variations are: I'm a godly man because I go to church every week, and I'm a good family man or woman because I don't believe in divorce.

I can't follow my inner voice if I'm trying to do what's right or wrong. These are systems that conflict. The inner voice leads us to our truth and puts us in harmony with the higher power and most people around us. Following the laws, so I can be right or wrong, just leads to confusion as far as I can see. So that's why it's necessary to choose between the two systems of right and wrong or the inner voice because they can't be used at the same time.

It isn't that the inner voice leads to wrong, it doesn't. But in the short run it may seem to. The inner voice may lead you to some things that don't seem right by conventional logic. For example, you may be led to follow some things that are good for you, but don't seem to be doing much for someone else. Later you find that you were the one who needed something and by getting it you became a better person and it worked out to be very much for the good. You look back and marvel at it a little and say, "How did that work out so well?" But it just did. And it worked in a way we just couldn't have figured out ahead of time.

How do I think the system works? I think there are universal laws of the emotions and the spirit just as there are on the material plans. When you drop something, it falls. When you have resentment and bitterness it kills your life and eventually your body. When you do things seeking rewards and approval, nothing comes back. When you do good things quietly because of your own need, you get back far more than you gave. When you withhold your inner self from the people around you, they move away from you. When you open your inner self to the people around you, they move up close.

Aren't these laws like the laws of the religious systems? Very much so. But you can establish the validity of those laws for yourself and follow them independently of a religious system. Where does the observance of these laws lead? At first, they give more freedom from our compulsions; our lives are not so unmanageable. In the cases of people who have been practicing these ideas for a long time, I see them living a spirit-guided life where they have turned their wills and their lives over to the care of God as they understand Him. I see in their lives a beautiful demonstration of the very essence of Christ's teaching: peace, love, gentleness, and compassion for themselves and others. This is so striking to me because these people used to lead lives of the most destructive self-centeredness.

Many people are afraid to put aside "right" and "wrong" and seek truth. They feel that if they removed themselves from the threat and the punishment of "right" and "wrong" they would do terrible things. I know of that fear and it is a great comfort to me to see how groundless it is. When people seek truth guided by the spirit they do a better job of following the principles and guidelines than before. They stop some of their lying, cheating, and stealing. After a while I see that they not only obey most of the written laws, they rise above them and learn to truly love themselves and their neighbors.

A strict observance of the law really isn't worth much in a life. All it does is keep you out of jail. It is when a person can meet the law and go beyond it into the law of love that really good things happen in their lives. And when you live the law of love, I've seen that you don't break the written laws.

But the law of love is a very frightening law to live because it is so indefinite and uncertain. How can you know what is the loving thing to do? It is hard. How can you be certain you won't be wrong? You can't. You can just follow the spirit as well as you can. You know you will make some mistakes but you will usually be able to see your mistakes and correct them before too much harm is done.

But doesn't that mean that at times you will look like a fool to other people? And the answer is yes, you will. Even more often you will look like a fool to yourself. But as you develop your ability to follow the spirit your faith grows as you see what good changes have been produced in your life.

I see more and more clearly that man has three parts that are hooked into one. He has a body, a mind with emotions and will, and then he has a spirit. The small, quiet inner voice of the spirit sits inside every person I've ever met waiting to be heard. I see that until I was ready to listen to that spirit my life was a chaos. No human power of the mind or body could manage my life. But the spirit could. All I had to do was let it guide me.

I believe we are spiritual beings and that the spiritual part of us is the constructive voice to follow because it serves the best interests of the mind-body-spirt combination. The spirit voice leads us to truth that builds and restores the body and clears the mind. When we follow the self-centered voice of the ego, it speaks just for the body and mind. But because the voice of the ego serves its own needs it is not in harmony with the best for the body-mind and does not meet the needs of the unified mind-body-spirit. So the body breaks down and the mind grows confused. We need to follow the spirit as the head of the body. When we try to make either the rational mind or the body the leader, the whole system breaks down.

This is to me the weakness of the psychological systems. Almost all of them deny the spirit part of man. Psychology has just newly broken away from philosophy and it wants to be a big boy and go it on its own, which means accepting mind and body but not spirit.

When I observed that, for the people in AA, you couldn't get long-term contented sobriety without a higher power, the spirit part, I could see that you had to have a higher power in your psychological system or it wouldn't work. Here is alcoholism, the problem that medicine and psychiatry have been completely helpless with. Medicine works on the body and psychiatry on the mind. What is different about AA is that it also works on the spirit as well as mind-body.

After five years of sobriety, an old friend of mine in AA said to his sponsors: "How come I'm just sober and miserable, instead of sober and happy like some of those who've been around longer?" What they told him was, "That's because you haven't been willing enough to go into the higher power part of the program." So hard as it was for him, he went as deep as he could into that side of the program.

"But," you ask, "couldn't it be that alcoholics and other people in the various twelve-step programs are very different people who have some kind of authority problem and so have a need for solving that through a higher power?" That could be. But something I've seen about psychology is that if it doesn't work for one pigeon, it can't work for all of them. If it does work for one pigeon, chances are it will work for all of them. I know people are just a little bit more complicated than pigeons, but I see too much truth about myself in the pigeon and rat research to argue how much more complicated I am than they are.

Our society is one of the few I know of that systematically excludes spiritual matters from consideration. We have lost that whole natural language of the spirit that still exists with the American Indian and Eastern religions plus some of the Pentecostals. Our country today does not have freedom of religion in the universities and intellectual circles. Religion and the spiritual quest are scorned not openly but even worse indirectly. Spiritual questions are seen as being beneath contempt. They're not even worthy of discussion outside of a philosophy class. So we don't have freedom of religion at the universities, we have open contempt and opposition—the same closed minds the professors criticize in religion.

Yet, I found students at the universities I have taught at or given speeches to, to be spiritually hungry, even starved. I could talk to them all day long about things of the spirit. As long as I avoided denominational terms, God-talk, I could count on an eager, attentive audience.

What I've just discussed is the very heart of this book. We all know that body-mind are all hooked together and are interdependent. But when we're relying on one of those two parts to be the leader and excluding the true leader, the third part of the body—the inner voice of the spirit—then there is no way we can have harmony in ourselves. And when we aren't in harmony with ourselves, there's no way we can be in harmony with life. When we will accept the spirit part of ourselves and let it lead, then we can have harmony with ourselves. As the effect of following that spirit changes our lives, we can begin to see what wonders we each are. And then we can see what wonders the others around us are.

So we can either continue in our self-centered way or we can move to a higher power–centered way of life where we are in harmony with the higher power and the people around us. But to do this we have to go against most schools of thought in psychology. Psychology is the science of controlling behavior. Usually the behavior we want to control is our own. But how can we find a psychology system that will openly recognize the inner voice and tell us how to follow it instead of the voice of the ego—the self-centered voice?

The only psychological systems I know of that were, as they developed, fairly open to guidance from above and without were Carl Jung's, Viktor Frankl's and Roberto Assagioli's.

Back in Jung's and Freud's day, as now, there was a terrible resistance on the part of psychology and psychiatry to matters of the spirit. There is a story about Jung that is such a beautiful example of this problem.

In 1931 Jung was treating an American, Roland H., for his alcoholism and other problems. After a year of treatment he felt he was all right but soon after he started in drinking again. When he went back to Switzerland, Jung told him of his hopelessness as far as any further medical or psychiatric treatment might be concerned.

When Roland asked if there was any other hope, Jung told him there might be if he could become the subject of a spiritual or religious experience—a genuine conversion that might reorder his personality when nothing else could.

Roland joined the Oxford movement, which emphasized self-survey, confession, restitution, the giving of oneself in service of others, meditation and prayer.

In those surroundings Roland did find a conversion experience that released him from his compulsion to drink.

Roland H. told Edwin T., who then also had spiritual experience, and Edwin T. told his friend Bill W., who was a hopeless alcoholic. A little later Bill W. was hospitalized for his alcoholism and accidentally saw on his chart that his family doctor had written that there was no hope for him, a mental hospital or death were his only alternatives.

As the story is told in *Grapevine*, the AA magazine, "Bill W. knelt by his bed and cried out in despair. If there be a God, will he show himself. He immediately had an illumination of enormous impact and dimension and he was released from the alcoholic obsession. He was a free man and went on to co-found AA."[3]

Bull W. in a letter he wrote to Carl Jung in 1961 told of the crucial part Jung's conversation with Roland H. had played in the formation of AA.

Jung wrote back to Bill W. a week later. Remember that this was in 1961 and Jung was eighty-six and in the last year of his life. Jung's letter is so important that I'll quote it completely.

"Dear Mr. W.

Your letter has been very welcome, indeed.

I had no news from Roland H. any more and often wondered what has been his fate. Our conversation which he has adequately reported to you had an aspect of which he did not know. The reason that I could not tell him everything was that those days I had to be exceedingly careful of what I said. I had found out that I

[3] AA *Grapevine*, January 1968, p. 17, letter from Bill W. to Carl Jung and Jung's reply.

was misunderstood in every possible way. Thus, I was very careful when I talked to Roland H. But what I really thought about, was the result of many experiences with men of his kind.

His craving for alcohol was the equivalent, on a low level, of the spiritual thirst of our being for wholeness, expressed in medieval language: The Union with God.* How could one formulate such an insight in a language that is not misunderstood in our days?

The only right and legitimate way to such an experience is, that it happens to you in reality and it can only happen to you when you walk on a path which leads you to higher understanding. You might be led to that goal by an act of grace or through a personal and honest contact with friends, or through a higher education of the mind beyond the confines of mere rationalism. I see from your letter that Roland H. has chosen the second way, which was, under the circumstances, obviously the best one.

I am strongly convinced that the evil principle prevailing in this world leads the unrecognized spiritual need into perdition, if it is not counteracted either by real religious insight or by the protective wall of human community. An ordinary man, not protected by an action from above and isolated in society cannot resist the power of evil, which is called very aptly the Devil. But the use of such words arouses so many mistakes that one can only keep aloof from them as much as possible.

* "As the hart panteth after the water brooks, so panteth my soul after thee, O God." (Psalm 42:1)

These are the reasons why I could not give a full and sufficient explanation to Roland H. But I am risking it with you because I conclude from your very decent and honest letter that you have acquired a point of view above the misleading platitudes one usually hears about alcoholism.

You see, "alcohol" in Latin is "spiritus" and you use the same word for the highest religious experiences as well as for the most depraving poison. The helpful formula therefore is: Spiritus contra spiritum.

Thanking you again for your kind letter
　　　　　I remain
　　　　　　yours sincerely
　　　　　　　C. G. Jung"

Here is one of the greatest men in psychiatry and in 1931 and again in 1961 he dared not speak his true feelings openly because of the risks of being misunderstood and distorted by his fellow psychoanalysts.

And the climate is still the same today. When I presented a paper discussing the part of the higher power in curing the alcoholic to the Montana Psychological Association some of my fellow scientists would not even read my paper. At the sight of the words "higher power" they turned over the paper. Now scientists aren't supposed to do that. We have an obligation to look at the evidence offered in support of any argument. But higher power propositions in most psychological groups I have seen are either not even entertained or they are dismissed with scorn as being beneath contempt and not worth discussion.

I am fortunate in that I am pretty free of institutional

psychology. I don't need their money and I don't need their approval so I can pretty much say what I feel. But even more important, I can see that I have my own life to save and the lives of the people in my family are involved. So I'm anxious to find the most powerful psychology I can find without thoughts of where I should or shouldn't look. My training as an experimental psychologist has made me look for evidence of what works and then let the theory come out of what works. If the theory comes first in some area, then I want to see good evidence to support that theory.

I'm not saying that this is any divine truth handed down from on high. I'm saying this is a psychological system that you can test for yourself out there in life. It's just like the little green Martian trying to figure out what rules we drive by. He comes to the stop sign and when the sign is red, he had better stop or he will get hit. You try that and see. About ninety-nine per cent of the time you won't get hit. When the light is green, it says you can go through the intersection carefully, watching in both directions for the one out of a hundred times when some nut is going to come through the red light that's guarding you.

This is a psychological system that works pretty well, especially considering the humanity of the people running it. You can verify that. I didn't get it handed down from on high. I didn't discover it, I uncovered it lying out there in life. The man-made psychological systems are defective because they were, in a sense, invented, part of them, not derived completely experimentally from life. Part of the reason for the weaknesses in most psychological systems is that, as I mentioned, most psychologists have a tremendous prejudice against any kind of higher power. And they don't want to put that in their system and that makes

107

their system defective. But psychologists aren't supposed to be prejudiced (which means prejudging). They are supposed to be scientists and scientists aren't supposed to be prejudiced against anything when it comes to their science. You've got to admit anything into your system that works. If it works you've got to put it in. If it doesn't work, you've got to throw it out.

I have seen, through careful and wide-ranging observation, that alcoholics can't get contented, long-term sobriety without recognizing a higher power of some kind. That shows that on one of the toughest kind of psychological problems to solve, which psychiatrists and psychologists and ministers are terrible at, you need a higher power in your system. You've got to have a higher power in your system or it won't work.

I have seen the same thing in less tough problems like the kind you and I face. They aren't really less tough; they just look less tough. In those problems I've seen you've also got to have a higher power in your system or it won't work very well.

If you're at the center, I guarantee your system is going to break down. I guarantee it. I can tell you ahead of time the problems you're going to have. Now, am I some smart aleck who is able to read your mind? No. I have seen all kinds of people who have built their own psychological system with themselves at the center and I know pretty well the problems that you find with that kind of system.

Each of us are inclined to think philosophers and psychologists are people with lofty educations and people very separated from us. But that's not so. It is impossible for each of us to avoid having a philosophy of life. Our philosophy is the things we feel are important in life. Our psychology is the system we use to control our own behavior and the behavior of the people around us. If I use my anger to control people that's part of my own psychological system. If I use making people feel sorry for me or feel sorry for myself, that's my own psychological system that I use in an attempt to control life.

There is no way we can avoid having a psychological system, and there is almost no way we can avoid being influenced by the systems of the major psychologists. The influence of Freud, Pavlov, Jung, Adler, Perls, Berne, Rogers, Maslow, etc. permeate the culture we live in and variations of their systems are being used by so many of the people around us.

So, like a fish, we are afloat in a sea of psychologies. That's why it is such a problem to us that there is this terrible resistance in most psychological schools to the higher power that can change personality and the inner voice that can guide us to a clearer sense of our inner perfection.

Someone once said that science is too important to be left to the scientists. The same holds true for psychology. Your personal psychology is too important to be left to any psychologist I've ever met yet. Your psychology has to come from you. You can draw from the popular psychologists and from the personal psychologies of people you admire. But there is no way you can avoid making choices as to the individual points you will include or throw out of the system you use in your daily life.

Notice I'm not talking about the system you talk about using or claim you use. I've seen all kinds of people who claim they believe in the various psychologies who actually use a totally different homemade system in their daily life.

One of the crucial decisions you have to make about your personal psychological system is: Do you believe for you that there is any power outside yourself? Or, are you all the power there is? Do you believe for you that there is an inner voice deep inside you that can be a reliable guide to you in life? And do you believe that the voice of the self-centered self has often led you into things that weren't good for you? If you believe in the higher power and the inner voice, then you have the basis for a very different psychology from what is commonly written of.

It's not that the higher power and inner voice are completely omitted in modern psychology. The basic idea in Carl Rogers' client-centered therapy is that each client has his own answer within him waiting to be found. Isn't that quite like an inner voice?

My inner voice is prepared to give me good guidance. All I need to do is strip away all my intellectual and self-centered objections and trust that little inner voice. It has led me to all the good things in my life. My self-centered voice has led me to most of the trouble in my life. You would think, with that kind of experience, that there would be no question which way I would go.

But it is so hard to follow that inner voice because I don't know where it is taking me. I'm not in control. I was in San Francisco speaking recently. In the summer the fog comes rolling in off the bay and cools down the city in the daytime and then goes rolling back to the sea. I told the group I was speaking to that following the inner voice was like walking in the edge of the fog bank as it rolled back. It is perfectly clear behind me and I can see where I have been. But it is so foggy in front of me that I can't see more than a step or two at a time. I hear the ocean roaring ahead of me as it smashes against the cliffs and I'm afraid. But I look back and see I've come through some very difficult places with no problem. So I need just to keep on walking a step at a time.

As old Heinze Koppes said to me in Switzerland, "I walk most safely if I don't know where I go." That's very hard to do even when I've done quite a lot of it. It was so hard to do at first that I nearly had to be killed three times to make me start. But more and more I can see that the inner voice is my true guidance system.

FIVE

Healing the Emotional Chaos
in the Subconscious

Think of the kindest, most beautiful person you've ever met, and by beauty I mean inner beauty. In that person it probably wasn't hard to see their inner perfection. Now think of the most angry, awful, disgusting person you've ever met. That person, too, had the same inner perfection in them. The only problem was the second person's inner perfection was so crusted over with a storm of emotions and the consequences that you couldn't see their inner perfection.

Why do I say this? It is because some of the most beautiful people I've ever met came out of some of the lowest parts of society. They were on skid rows, in prison and mental institutions, beat their wives, even raped their own daughters. Yet now these people are the sweetest, happiest people I've ever seen. They're certainly far happier than any church group I've ever been around. So buried deep in those individuals, while they looked so terrible, was their inner perfection, which now shows clearly. That's why I don't question that there is an inner perfection in each of us no matter how down we are on ourselves or how bad an appearance we present.

How do we get to our inner perfection? We have to go way deep into the self, down into the subconscious mind using the guidance of our inner voice. It's like our inner perfection was a rare jewel buried deep inside us and to get to it we have to go through obstacles like savage animals and nightmare scenes of what we are or what we fear we are. We have to see our deep emotions and own up to them as our own. We have to plumb the subconscious and see our darkest deeds, thoughts, and feelings and take responsibility for them. We have to admit that we did those things, thought those thoughts, and had those feelings. No devil made us do it. We did it.

When we get through all those thoughts, feelings, and deeds that lie temporarily buried in the subconscious, we can get to the jewel of our inner perfection. And miraculously most of the crap we waded through to get inside ourselves melts away and it's possible for a few people to love us and see our inner perfection, too. And our subconscious becomes less a prison for bad thoughts and more of a positive, creative force in our lives.

Many things keep us from this deep self-acceptance. We fear what we will see because we've all taken a quick peek deep into ourselves once in a while and we didn't like what we saw. Another problem is we're trying to use someone else's rules for our search instead of finding our own rules. But we have only the inner voice to guide us and we have to find the rules that are right for us and put aside all the "I shoulds" and "I must do's" that bind us and keep us from finding a higher set of rules where we do lovely things because we want to instead of because we have to.

In the acceptance lies the solution. And the solution seems like such a paradox because we have to accept all the things we don't like about our feelings and our past deeds before we can get to something better.

Self-acceptance is not such a paradox when we see life is like a river. Self-acceptance is like seeing there is a current in the river. When we float with the river, we go fast without effort. That's what we're talking about. We're trying to figure out what are the laws of life.

I found that in the old days I was following the wrong set of laws. I was breaking most all the written laws, like I was always speeding. I was also offending the universal laws. But I fooled myself by having a bunch of other laws that I did a real good job of obeying.

I thought it was a law that you're not supposed to be different from anybody else. You're supposed to conform, dress like everybody else. Would somebody show me where that law is written down some place? Or show me evidence that obeying it leads to a better life for me? I thought people wouldn't like me if I was different. Please show me where that's written down.

People argue they have been taught to conform. There have been many in this country who begged people to be individualists and gave us a good example of their individualism to follow. Why didn't I listen to them instead of the person who preached conformity to me? I followed all the wrong laws and broke all the written and univeral laws I shouldn't have broken.

Okay, so we say we're going to get it all together. We're always trying to do that. What that means is we're going to be in control. That's scaling this beautiful world down to a nice little boxlike system that we can handle.

But we have a difficulty. We start making a few changes, we put a patch in our life. Then, when things seem reasonably under control again, we say we have it all together. But we never have it all together, we should never try.

Getting it all together is the exact opposite of surrender and that's what we're talking about, surrendering to the harmony of life. You don't have to have any religion. You can forget it all and just surrender to the harmony of life and it will work.

Some religious people write to me, "Jess, if you would accept Jesus Christ as your personal savior you wouldn't have all those problems that you have. You'd be a nice, beautiful person like me." And I want to say, "If you're such a beautiful person, how come you're causing me so much pain at this moment?" And the sadness is the theologians won't support that follower of their religion.

My good friend Dr. Bruce Morgan says it isn't that easy. Even in Christianity, old Paul, who had been a Christian for fifteen years and was one of the head Christians, was still having troubles. There were things he felt he should do but he could not do them. There were things he knew he wasn't supposed to do but he did them. That's honesty.

So here's Paul, the first of the big-shot Christians and after fifteen years of practice, he was still having trouble with the guy in the top control room fighting the guy in the lower control room. And occasionally the guy in the bottom control tower would take over and Paul would see himself doing things he didn't want to do.

I know that this Christian who writes me is honestly concerned for my welfare when he says, "If you'd just accept Christ as your personal savior, you'd never have a problem again." I know he doesn't realize he is flying right in the face of one of his chief teachers, Paul. He's distorting his religion just as he distorted his earlier life and now he seems to me to be trying to find certainty and control because of his fear and lack of faith. His fear keeps him from seeing what's going wrong in his own life and his lack of faith keeps him from seeing that there will be people close to me to correct me and chastise me when I need it.

The theologians say that we have a spiritual awakening and that's the beginning of a lifetime growth and a walk that is the Christian way. That's their terminology. Now you don't need to use it. I have seen that people do unbelievably beautiful things guided only by their higher power—God as they understand him. So I don't care how bad your experiences have been with religion, you don't need all those words. I know from experience that the spirit is the crucial part, not the words. You can take a higher power, God as you understand him, as your universal principle. You can use that your whole life long and it will get you out of the soup, through the problems to where eventually you're no offense to yourself or the people around you. To me that's a beautiful thing. I'm sure it's beautiful to be inside that kind of a body. And it's beautiful to be around. People like that live a happy life and a very long life, that's another interesting thing about it.

Of course what it shows is if you don't want to die, it's amazing how long you live. And when you want to die, it's equally amazing how quickly you can get out of this life. It's very simple to get out. Six to eighteen months after a terrible disaster like the death of a spouse, a lot of cancer comes. Did disaster cause the cancer? Not directly, no. The disaster hits the mind and the mind's troubles stir up the body and disturb the body's immunological system

116

and that lets cancer flare up that was there all the time. I would guess that everybody's got cancer in them but their immunological system holds it down. Cold sores come from viruses just as cancer does. I've seen people pop out with cold sores on their lips in less than an hour after some terribly upsetting event.

We were taught that the intellect was power, all the power there was. That's a wrong teaching. Our so-called rational mind deceives us constantly. For example, we tell the kids not to take dope for their neurosis while we take dope for our neurosis. Don't smoke grass but it's okay to stay zonked on Valium like I do.

In the Serenity Prayer, it says, "God, grant me the serenity to accept the things I cannot change, courage to change the things I can and the wisdom to know the difference." What does this wisdom to know the difference tell me about the things I can't change? An awful lot of things about myself, as I mentioned earlier, I can't change. If I can't change it then I better accept it. Do something.

If I've been waging war against my finger that snakes out into the open peanut butter jar, and if I'm not going to beat it, I'll join it. And I'll say, "Finger, go to it. I'll lug around whatever fat you put on me. If I can't beat you, I'll join you." Otherwise I won't even enjoy the peanut butter because I won't even know I ate the stuff, my mind is so closed to what I'm doing. What fun is that? I get the fat and I don't get the fun. That's the worst possible outcome. Most overweight people have no idea how much and how often they eat. It seems like they're lying to the people around them, but they aren't really. They're blind to their own eating. So acceptance of eating is a giant step forward compared to blindness to it.

Now some of you may think I'm a cop-out, just a

worthless low immoral person and you're probably right. I'd counsel those of you who are inclined to feel that way to avoid me from here on because I'm sure it's going to get worse and I'm going to be more of a bad influence on you. My mother didn't know it, but I was the kind of kid she didn't want me to play with. My God, some of the things I did. My mother always said it was these other kids that were the bad influence on me. My dear mother, I owe her a lot for that.

In my egotism I used to try to change all kinds of things that couldn't be changed by me. The crisis came when that ran out. I remember a lady who sat in my class, a young woman about thirty. She said, "Jess, what do you mean when you say you're powerless over your emotions? I'm not powerless over my emotions." She had just been divorced by a guy who didn't want to live with her any more. She was going with a guy who had a wife out East but he was already telling her, "I love you, honey, but I don't want to marry you." And she was having trouble with her kids and she was drinking too much. But she was not powerless over her emotions. She had them nicely under control.

I'm suggesting, you see, that I could look at myself if I were in her spot and say, "Hey, Jess, your husband couldn't stand you. That means you aren't 100 per cent lovable to all people. This new guy doesn't want to marry you either, so that says you aren't 100 per cent lovable to him. The fact you need so much alcohol to drown your pain isn't a real good sign but we'll have to drown our pain any way we can and I guess that's one way." Okay, that's the way it is. So the minute you see your situation honestly, you're started.

This is essentially what the alcoholic does. He accepts the fact he needs alcohol to drown his pain. All he de-

118

cides is that he is not going to use alcohol this five minutes to drown his pain. He doesn't say he will never drink alcohol again. My God, nobody can control the whole rest of their life. But he is capable of saying, "In the next five minutes I won't use alcohol to drown my pain." We scale life down to things we can handle and we can't always handle them and so the alcoholic has a slip. In that five minutes he didn't do a job. But he just puts that failure aside and tries to find the power to get him through the next five minutes.

We can't fight the world. When we try, we fail, because when I'm fighting the world, I'm playing God. I'm asking the world to revolve around me as the center point. And when I'm at the center point my world breaks down at the center. When my higher power is at the center point, my world does not break down at the center and I can take a vacation once in a while. I don't need to sleep with my feet in the air to keep the sky from falling. I get days off. We all like days off.

Now there are some crises in my life that I don't cause but they aren't crises if I'm in tune. When I get up in the morning, and it's raining, I can see it as a crisis or get in tune. Everybody around me, everybody I love is going to die, many of them before me. I can't tell you how many friends I've buried in the ten years I've been in Bozeman. An awful lot of those folks were supposed to live way longer than me. And they're gone. But you see I didn't cause those things so I don't need to get all tied up in them. And yes, I will miss those people, but there are other good people around.

There is a beautiful scene in *The Great Gatsby* where Rosenthal the big gambler is sitting with Gatsby and his friend. Rosenthal told them his friend was being buried that day and his funeral parade was just going by.

119

Gatsby's friend said, "Aren't you going out?" and the guy said, "No. We had a good time together when he was around."

Is this total resignation? Is this determinism? No. It means being active where we can be. These were the people Viktor Frankl tells us about, those who managed to live in the concentration camps. They did what they could. The way I read his book, the first key to their survival was their acceptance of the concentration camp. They didn't pretend they were somewhere else. They didn't even spend a lot of time wishing they were somewhere else or blaming the past. They accepted where they were and made the very best of their life in those terrible circumstances.

I think it was out of this acceptance that they were able to do the other thing Frankl talks about, which was to see some meaning in life that helped produce the acceptance. But whatever, there was in those who lived an acceptance of their daily life that helped them transcend that daily life and rise above it. That was one of the toughest of all the trials our generation ever had. But all that did, in exaggerated scale, was speed up the process we see around us in life. You can die of cirrhosis of the liver at thirty or thirty-five depending on how much you can drink or how weak your liver is. All the concentration camp does is squeeze things like that into a shorter time. It's like speeding up a motion picture so you can see how it ends sooner. It's the same process.

One of my students in the early days of my teaching said, "Jess, my God, what if I looked at myself in deep acceptance and found I was a sex maniac?" I know the answer to that question now. I'm a sex maniac, too, partly. I've also got some lovely qualities. They're all mixed together. But you say, my God, I couldn't stand looking at such a kaleidoscope, now you see one thing, and then another. And still another. That isn't a great human being I'm seeing. But who says it isn't?

What you're wanting to see in your kaleidoscope is an integrated human god. That's what I had in mind being; a 100 per cent perfect god. I might allow myself a few small imperfections like I might swear once a year, just a couple of imperfections, just enough to make me human. Well, whoever put me together didn't put me together that way. "Well," you say, "what an awful thing." The answer is, "Maybe." But whatever. These are the feelings I spoke about at the beginning of the chapter. This is the stuff we have to go through to find that inner perfection that lies inside.

So I've found I've got two choices when it comes to my imperfections. I can fight them or I can join them. I can fight my personality or I can join it. What I've decided is it works a lot better when I join it than when I fight it. One of my students made a beautiful statement of self-acceptance: "God made me and God don't make junk."

A great way to handle an itch is to scratch it. "It will never work," you say. Well, that's lack of faith. It does work. It works better than the alternative. You sit there saying, "I'm not going to scratch that itch." That itch has got you. You think you're free but you're not. I'm free at least part of the time, the rest of the time I'm scratching itches. I've got a lot more freedom now than when I didn't scratch an itch.

There is a beautiful story in Paul Rep's book *Zen Flesh, Zen Bones* about the two Zen monks who went to the village. It had rained for days and the streets were ankle-deep in mud. A pretty young woman was standing on the walk considering how to get across the street. One of the monks went over, picked her up, and carried her across the street. The other monk was silent the rest of the day. That evening he said, "We monks don't go near females, especially not young and lovely ones. It is dangerous. Why did you do that?"

"I put that girl down this afternoon," said the first monk. "Are you still carrying her?"

This is the trap we fall into when we let an itch dominate us. Many church people are violently obsessed with dirty books. All day long they carry dirty passages from dirty books around in their minds. They argue they are trying to clean up the world. But it is a shame they have to carry so much of that dirt around in their own minds.

I used to wonder how come so many people around me were phonies and now I'm not around many phonies any more. You know why? Simple. In the old days I used to pretend all the time I was something I wasn't. Then I bitched because I attracted people who were pretending to be something they weren't and I thought this world was sure full of phonies. Now that I've quit pretending most of the time I'm not trying to be something I'm not. As much as possible I'm trying to be what I am. Now I'm attracting a lot of people who like what they see and who are trying to be what they are. And so I don't see hardly any phonies any more. Where did all the phonies go? Isn't that funny?

I'm an old advertising man and I see now what happened was very simple. I advertised for a certain kind of person and that's what I got. I was advertising for people who wanted to make money and impress other people. And then I was complaining about the kind of people my advertising was attracting. Now I'm running a different kind of advertisement. I'm saying, "Hey, you derelicts of the world out there, here is a fellow sufferer." And the derelicts of the world are flocking to me. I'm very big with people in prisons and mental hospitals. Any of you model citizens better not hang around me too long because it will hurt your flawless reputation, it will be guilt by association.

I was giving a seminar with Elisabeth Kübler-Ross a year ago last summer. There were a bunch of ministers and divinity students at this seminar on death, dying, and living. That was to be my part, the living. And those ministers in their introductions alluded to how they had things pretty well in hand. They did admit to a couple of small imperfections. This one divinity student said she thought she had everything in the ministry figured out but then she realized she didn't understand dying so she was there to finish that and complete her education. And there were a lot of other people who were just helping people a lot.

By the time they got through introducing themselves the load of virtue and the odor of sanctity was so heavy in that room, I could hardly stand it. I was so mad I said terrible things to those folks. Some of those ministers wouldn't speak to me for the next two and a half days. Honest to God, they would not talk to me. They would move away when I came down the hall. And I wanted to say to them, "Hey, you guys, I'm big with the derelicts that you are wanting to minister to. How are you going to manage to skip across somebody like me to get to those derelicts? How come you can't relate to this derelict?"

But I was in the wrong crowd for me. So I went crazy and showed them and me a side of my personality none of us liked to see. I don't have a firm enough sense of my being and enough confidence in that being to be the same person no matter what crowd I'm in. So mama was right after all. I should watch out who I run with. She just didn't understand that sometimes it's ministers I should stay away from and drunks I should be with. That's why it's so important for me to use honest advertising so I can attract the people who are right for me and avoid attracting people who are wrong for me. And again, when I see myself go crazy like I did with some of the ministers, it shows me how powerless over my emotions I still am.

I spoke to a group some years ago in Minneapolis. Afterward, I noticed a lady hanging around the fringes wanting to talk to me. After I finished talking to some people I started down the hall and she came after me. "Jess," she said, "I've got a problem." I asked, "How long has it been going on?" She said, "About a year. It's the other husband in our bridge foursome. How do I stop it?"

"You can't."

"What do you mean I can't?"

"If you could stop, you would have. Tell me about the friends you can open your heart to."

"Well, there's my mother."

"You can't tell her this so she doesn't count."

"Well, I've got this other friend."

"That's better than nothing. What about your kids?"

"I've given them everything."

"Right. That's the problem. You feel you've given them everything and you didn't get anything and now the little girl is out running around saying, 'To heck with you, old gal, you aren't going to do anything for me. And I'm fleeing this setup of yours regularly because I've been sitting here without any nourishment for so long and I can see if I live with you on your rules I'm not ever going to get any. So I'm fleeing.' "

"How am I going to get that little girl to stay at home?"

"Start doing some good things for her, getting some

124

real friends, some intimate friends she can trust. And opening your heart so you can have some mutual relationships and have some real communications and good things coming into your system."

"That would take a lot of time."

"Right."

The first couple of times I ran into her after that she lied to me and said things were really going great. She later wrote and admitted things were just rocking along; the only improvement was she was accepting it better.

I finally got the last chapter in that particular story. She recently wrote me and said the little girl was back home, she wasn't sleeping with the guy any more and the bridge foursome was still going strong. So with a healthy dose of acceptance and patience which let her little girl out to play for a while and bringing some good things to her life it only took six years of playing before the little girl came back home.

You might think that story isn't a very good advertisement for acceptance but I like the ending a lot better than many stories that I've heard of. One way most people say you should handle a problem like that is to say "no" to your little girl. You can do that but the only problem is that the little girl dies of a broken heart and there's no life left in the body. So the body soon dies, too. Understand, I'm not saying that there was only one thing she could do for her little girl. She could have said to her little girl, "You can't sleep with the other guy, but I will find another way you can get some love in your life by opening up to my husband." But the point is something had to be done and what the lady did was sure a lot better than nothing.

A young gal I know was deep in the Pentecostal movement. She got with a guy and ended up sleeping with

125

him. It was bothering her going to the Holy Spirit meetings because she was sleeping with this guy and she felt bad. And she wanted to get rid of him. She would go to one of these Pentecostal meetings and come home. When the guy would get her in bed, he'd laugh at her, "Ha, ha, look what you're doing right after your meeting." And that made her feel bad, but she didn't leave. Finally she left. After a year she got a message from God to come back and see this guy.

I said, "Linda, honey, I don't think that was God talking, that was your hormones." And she said all the old stuff was going on again. I said, "Well, Linda, just live with the guy and go to your meetings."

"Oh," she said, "I couldn't, Jess."

I said, "Why not?"

"What will people think?"

I said, "Aha, that's the problem, isn't it, little one? What will people think? Not what will God think or what does Linda think, but what will people think?" So Linda's little girl was out playing and the Holy Spirit part of her was just aghast at what this little girl was doing with her time, so much of the time. So she had to go into hypocrisy and lying and denial and all this other stuff. And that's a beautiful way to be blind to life.

I see the twelve steps as used by AA, EA, etc., as so powerful for two reasons. The first is the steps themselves. They contain, in a very simple form, a wonderful program that's so complete and deep that most people in twelve-step programs find they can spend the rest of their lives working on that simple program and gaining from it.

The twelve steps ask people to develop a god of their understanding instead of someone else's understanding. Then it is suggested that people turn their lives over to that god of their understanding one day at a time. It is also suggested that people take a moral inventory of themselves and admit to God, to themselves, and to another human being the exact nature of their wrongs. This gets the skeletons out of the closet and lets people see that they aren't nearly as bad or different from others as they've thought for all these years.

The twelve steps suggest people be ready to give up their defects of character so they can be removed by the higher power. Amends are to be made to people who have been harmed. A continuing personal inventory is taken so when something goes wrong it can be corrected immediately. Meditation is used so a knowledge of the higher power's will for the person can be found along with the power to carry it out. The last step of the program says: "Having had a spiritual awakening as a result of these steps, we tried to carry this message and to practice the principles in all our affairs."

As I mentioned, I'm not an alcoholic but I have had the good fortune to spend much of the last ten years around people who practice these steps. And I find they contain a powerful psychological system. The words god and higher power are terribly hard for intellectuals and people disillusioned with god. We intellectuals are so smart we always know so much more than any god. That's why, when a university professor goes into alcoholism, it's almost impossible to save him. He's so smart that you can't tell him anything.

The words "god" and "higher power" are very hard for the people raised with a vengeful god who had religion beaten into them or shoved down their throats. Many of these people at first leave out all the steps of the twelve that mention god. Later, when they can consider a higher power, they might make the group their higher power.

Often it's years before they can begin to have a god of their own understanding.

Psychologists and psychiatrists who have looked at these steps sometimes think AA is a fundamental religious movement because of their belief in a higher power and what that belief can do. They don't seem to be able to see they are hung up in a word problem. Most psychologists believe, like Carl Rogers, that the answer to the person's problems is inside the person. That's very close, it seems to me, to what AA teaches. It just uses different words. To say that a client has an answer to his problem inside him is not far from saying that through meditation a person can discover God's will for them using God in the special sense of God as you understand him rather than in the usual sense, which is God as someone else understands him.

The second reason the twelve steps are so powerful is because of the close-knit groups they produce. An AA group is a wonderful thing to watch and to be part of even if only occasionally. There is a closeness and acceptance there that is so deep and so warm that it hits many people new to the groups like an electric shock. In the warmth of that acceptance people open like a flower in the sunshine, and the deep level of caring for one another that people find in the groups is something most people seek their whole life and don't find. All you need to do to experience this for yourself is to find an open AA group in your town and go to it. Or see if there is one of the other twelve-step groups you might be interested in.

This closeness of the groups has led many psychologists and psychiatrists to charge that AA is just substituting a new addiction to the group for the old one to alcohol. That's like saying we're addicted to the supermarket because we go there so often. As near as I can see, most societies in the world value warmth and acceptance. When a person has been starved for this all his life, it shouldn't be a surprise to psychologists that when they find it, they would cling to it. That's not a dependence, that's common sense.

In my experience, we psychologists and psychiatrists are so messed up that we can't stand so much closeness on a continuing basis, much less value it. There hasn't been a lot of use of tests of emotions on psychologists, for we are hesitant to use our own tests on ourselves. But when the California Personality Inventory was being normed, psychology graduate students were found to rank just above San Quentin prison inmates in their emotional adjustment. I don't take that test very seriously, though, because medical students ranked at the top. I'm sure doctors are better adjusted than we psychologists but I can't believe they are at the top.

To me, the difficulty we psychologists have in accepting the power and closeness in an AA group is a tribute to that very power. In AA groups I see warmth, acceptance, and caring of encounter or sensitivity groups maintained on a continuous basis so new people can come in at any time and the group keeps on functioning for its long-term members. And all that's necessary for functioning is a list of the twelve steps and the people who want to practice them. No leader or wise one is needed. The group runs itself and provides its own leadership. And it's almost completely run on group consensus rather than on majority vote. In fact, if there has to be a vote that's a sign there isn't much of a consensus and it might be best to wait a while and allow some more time for discussion. But smooth-functioning groups like this are so uncommon, they are hard for most people to understand. They think there must be some kind of group coercion or oppression going on. Anyone who has watched the process knows differently.

Close-knit groups, like in AA, are so important because when a person is taking their life apart and trying to put it back together in a better way, they need the support of people who understand and appreciate what they are trying to do. Psychologists are quick to admit alcoholism or emotional problems are family and community problems. And they argue that the family or community needs to be changed. All AA groups do is provide a place where the individual can learn new behavior and then practice that behavior in a supportive atmosphere. Special AA groups are provided for husbands and wives (Alanon) and for children (Alateens). But from what I've seen in AA, the alcoholic can become sober even when no one around him changes. This to me is an important validation of the AA group and a proof of its efficiency.

Healing groups such as an AA group, some other type of twelve-step group, or any close association with like-minded people is so necessary for going deep into ourselves. As we go in search of our inner perfection, we see many strange horrifying things deep inside us that are very hard to handle. Often the support we get from a good group is all that sustains us as we first take some of the tough medicine of ourselves. But before we can go deep like that, we have to see that we are powerless over our emotions, that our lives are unmanageable.

If you want a true test to illustrate whether you're powerless over your emotions or not, watch yourself and your feelings carefully for the next week while you drive your automobile. There's nothing so guaranteed to give a truer test of our real personality than driving a car.

A guy had had some kind of deep religious experience and he was trying to live it. He pulled up behind a car and he was giving the driver of the car ahead of him a terribly bad time because he stopped. Then he found it was because they were trying to get a crippled lady out of the car. And he found it was his neighbor driving. He asked Dear Abby, "Why do I do such awful things as this when I'm behind the wheel of a car?" I think it's for the same reason he does those awful things other times, too.

It's just like the story about the guy who's got the bumper sticker, "Honk if you love Jesus." Somebody comes up behind him at a stop light and honks and he comes piling out of his car ready to kill the guy. "You so and so, can't you see that light's red?"

You may have some convincing arguments as to why you're not powerless over your emotions. But I have lost, long ago, all chance to argue that point. I am exceptionally powerless over my emotions.

We don't like to think about it, though, because we're so self-centered and think we should be able to do everything and if we're powerless, where are we going to get the power? That's when we see we can't do it alone and that there has to be a power greater than ourselves or we're whipped. So we turn to some power outside ourself. You can have all kinds of higher powers. I believe in a higher power that has all power. So I've got a real good higher power. Mine can do all kinds of good things for me.

Well, if we don't want to get some higher power to help us out of our dilemma, then we're stuck. We have worshiped mind and science, thinking they had the power, yet we see ourselves acting like spoiled little children, so it's simple. We can go mad and die or we can go find some power.

A counselor told the story of a joke a young boy, one of his clients, played on the world by withdrawing into himself when faced by authority. The counselor told that as the boy's joke. But maybe we should cry at a story like that instead of laughing because the boy got none of what he needed and wanted and that's the problem. That's what we've done, you see. We've withdrawn within ourselves into these little boxes to protect ourselves. And the shells we've built around ourselves have become our prisons. We've denied what we are. We've lied to ourselves so long it's almost impossible to know what the truth is.

If I lied to myself increasingly for twenty years, to myself and others, could I then, all of a sudden, start telling the truth 100 per cent the next morning? No. I can get out of practice at anything. The further I get out of practice, the longer it's going to take me to get back into practice. So I'm going to recover the virtue of honesty, the same way I left it, a day at a time. And I'm going to have to try to get a little more honest with myself each day. And, as I mentioned, each day I'm going to try to get my mind a little further off skid row.

Now that kind of destroys my image of myself as the all-wise, controlling one. Here I'm supposed to be a psychologist. I'm supposed to be a man of letters and education. And yet I'm talking to you plain with no fancy words. Some people criticize my language. "Ain't you had no education at all, you dummy?" And what I've got to say is, "Yes, I've had some education." "Well, then why don't you use the language better?" The answer I have to give is, "I know how to use the language better but I prefer not to because I'm in the business of trying to communicate with some people who have an important part to play in saving my life. When I'm drowning in the ocean and I need a life preserver, I don't say, "If it pleases you, would you please assist me by taking the life preserver off its attachments and throwing it in my vicinity." I yell, "Help." I'm here saving my life and this is no place to pussy foot around about the language and smoke screen it. I want to say as clearly as I can what I'm up to because, as I say, you people have a very important part to play in saving my life.

I think we do have a freedom and I think I abused it a great deal. I think man is the only thing that doesn't have to fit into his environment. A monkey can't act like anything but a monkey. A man can act like a monkey or a mule or even a jackass. Man doesn't want to fit in at first. He wants to change outward circumstances instead of changing his inward self. But isn't the environment the laws of life? Obeying the laws of life gets a man out of the center point. If other people don't choose to live in harmony with life, fine. I don't want to let their living out of harmony or what I see as maybe living out of harmony, distract me from trying to live in harmony with everything including them.

Kahlil Gibran says, "My friend, you and I shall remain strangers unto life and unto one another and each unto himself until the day when you shall speak and I shall listen deeming your voice my own voice and when I shall stand before you thinking myself standing before a mirror."

This is where we need mutual relationships. In *"I Ain't Well—But I Sure Am Better"* I told how important mutual relationships are in my life. In a mutual relationship I can be myself. And as I be myself in that mutual relationship, I come to see myself. So you are a clear mirror to me in which I see myself. It isn't this old idea that I see in you something of you reflected in me. The relationship serves as a clear mirror to me in which I can see myself. Besides serving as a mirror to me, your

133

love for me as I am gives me the courage to be myself and to look deeper into my being.

Now I see in a typical relationship that it serves as a mirror to the other person, too. His being able to say to me how he feels in his heart lets him see what he is.

How did we get so screwed up? We got this way by going deeply and completely into self, trying to be God and trying to be perfect. But it's like there are two voices in us, and it's a question of which voice we want to hear. There's the self-centered voice which is concerned with externals. The self-centered voice is concerned with how people will view us, how we will look, what's going to happen, what other people are going to do. The voice of the true self is concerned solely for us, what is right for us. And oddly enough, that is the true voice.

That seeming selfishness poses a problem for the people in the twelve-step programs. It seems like a very selfish program of just doing what is right for you. The only thing is that's the only thing that works out good for the people around you. When you find what is truly right for you rather than the self-centered voice, this is the thing that produces as Wally Minto says, "Natural results without frustration or effort." But our experience, because of living in that self-centered life so much, has been that all results come from terrible effort and frustration and strain. Nothing good comes without toil. I always thought that. I thought the harder I worked and the more misery I found the better. But I can see now that was wrong. That's a very wrong teaching. Good things come without toil.

Proust said about writing his poetry, "If it isn't easy, it's impossible." It is very easy for me to write these books. When I wrote the first one I thought, "I'll never have another." This is my fourth and now I've got two,

134

three, or four ahead of me that I can see dimly. They're like eggs in a hen's canal. The eggs are moving down the canal and at a given time they are in various stages of development. But I don't know which one is going to come next.

These things, my books are easy. But before, when I was trying to pretend I was an advertising agency account executive even though I had absolutely none of the characteristics, it was exceptionally difficult, nearly impossible. So I've experienced life both ways. I've experienced life swimming upstream and I've experienced life floating with the current. I get ten times as much done today as I used to. And today there is almost no effort and I feel good at the end of the day.

I used to come home and sink into that big easy chair with my face buried in the newspaper or a book and the family couldn't have pried me out of there with a stick of dynamite. I was wiped out 100 per cent, emotionally, physically, every day. And I was reading, not for the sake of reading, but purely for the sake of escape, to get away from people. I haven't sat in that chair depleted of energy like that more than a couple of times in the last two or three years. And that is such a change.

So when Minto says that natural results come without effort, I know exactly what he means. The only way we can get natural results is out of being what we really are and then doing whatever comes out of that being. And again most of us think, "But I'm nothing. If I was just being what I naturally am I'd be nothing! or I'd be bad." And of course there's no faith in that. And also no experience at being that. Because I've never seen anybody go be what they really are and not have some good results right away. It's just that we've spent so much time away from our being, living the opposite way, we just can't believe there is anything good in us.

For most of us, living in a false sense of self is all we've ever experienced, trying to be something we aren't. We've been trying to go one way and the whole universe flows the other way. It's like trying to drive the wrong way on a one-way street. It can be done but it doesn't work very well.

We have an inner perfection, same as the oak tree. The little acorn grows up to be an oak tree. The little tomato seed grows up to be a tomato. We take a packet of dry seeds and think nothing of sticking them in the ground. We're just smacking our lips, thinking of the harvest we're going to eat. How asinine. Here's just a bunch of dust that we're scattering along the row with complete faith we will have a crop of tomatoes soon. And yet here we are the most magnificent thing, in my view, that's ever been created, each of us. If we will just allow that being that's uniquely us to flower and bloom, the fruits will be far more beautiful than anything we can design ourselves. It's like my old friend says about the beautiful rolling hills and mountains behind his place: "No landscape gardener ever designed something like that." And no human being ever designed people as lovely as the ones who just let go trying and simply try to be themselves so their inner perfection could be revealed for all to see.

In my first book I talked about the power and glory and majesty that's in each of us when we allow ourselves to bloom. This book here goes back to some of those ideas. At first I was going to call this present book *"Jess, You Ain't the Doctor."* I have come to see there's a better title for it. Instead of putting the emphasis on the fact that I don't control the world, the emphasis should be on my own inner perfection as I'm coming to see it more because there are my wife and my kids and my five friends who think I'm really something. Recently, when I was in the presence of one of those friends, I was reminded of something Vince said: "Sometimes I think I'm a worm and then I think I'm a wonder." And so in the presence of that friend I said, "Ain't I a wonder—and ain't you a wonder, too?"

But it has taken me a long time to see that I had my eye on the hole instead of the doughnut. I had my eye on the imperfections so strong that I couldn't see much else. I had my eye on how my little lower control tower was putting me up on the sandbank. I had my eye on my imperfections so much that I couldn't see the total perspective of myself. I was distorting myself as I was out trying to impress other people. I twisted my being into any shape I thought would please others so much that I wasn't allowing myself to be what I was. And so I lost a grasp of what I truly was because it all starts there.

Fifteen years ago when I went in search of what I was, I wanted to find what my being was and be it. I wanted to find what I believed in and do it. And when I went in search of that, it was only then that I began to have any kind of good results. When I started teaching, I got a promotion every year for four years. I was half-time instructor, full-time instructor, assistant professor, and associate professor with tenure at the University of Minnesota just like that. And I didn't ask for one of the promotions. That's the kind of thing that happens to you when you are being what you are as directly as you can.

I can't guarantee you'll have exactly the same results I did. All I can guarantee is that you'll have good results. I've never seen it fail.

But we're in a position where we're afraid of all the bad things that are in us and they are the things we are bringing about. So of course we would have no faith in our inner perfection. We haven't experienced the fruits of it. A good way to verify this is, if we are really not afraid of something and we really feel it's all right, we don't think about it at all. But what we fear is what we bring about and that's where our energy is all tied up. So when we're afraid of being bad, then that's what we will be. It's only when we truly accept something as completely all right that we are subconsciously free of it.

We find there's sound basis for this. We can look at all kinds of people who have got all the same problems we've got and they're managing to live and they're lovely people. Everybody who was famous in the 1800s died so that means that even death is all right. So if all of the things we fear and all the things we are are all right, that solves about 90 per cent of our problems.

Now we're still going to have flat tires. And Wally Minto shows us a nice way to handle them. When you go out and see your tire is flat you're going to have to fix it. You can't just say that the problem is all right. You have to fix it. But all you need to do is say, "It's all right that I have a flat tire. Yes, I'm going to be late getting home but that's all right. Yes, my husband or wife is going to yell at me, but that's all right. They've got the right to yell at me if they want to." So you calmly go about fixing your flat tire. So when you say everything is all right, you solve 90 per cent of the problems because you've got nothing to do about them. The 10 per cent like flat tires that you've got something to do about, you say that's all right, too. And you save 90 per cent of the problem with that flat tire. You're whistling and happy, you fix the flat tire, put the stuff in the trunk, and go on home. And so the flat tire doesn't take away your happiness either. So it's a way of getting rid of 90 per cent in the first place and another 9

138

per cent of what remains, so that 99 per cent of your problem goes away when you say it's all right.

Now some of us have problems that are so overwhelming that we can't face them next week. And the answer is. Thank God you don't have to face them next week yet. If you have to face them this week and next week and the week after all at once, you'd probably kill yourself. But you don't have to do that. All you have to do is get through the next five minutes. That's all you've got to do and most everybody can manage that.

So if you fear an unhappy marriage that's what you really believe in. Once you accept it, it's all right. As I mentioned earlier, when we worry, we insult God. Abdullah told me that and he wasn't even a Christian. When we worry, we insult God.

"But," you say, "if I let that little girl loose, you don't know what she would do." And the answer is, "You'd be surprised. I bet I do." And if that's something you need to do that bad then you better go do it. Because one way to control the little boy or little girl is to pat him on the head and say, "Hey, little honey, I hear you talking. I understand your feeling. I know what you want to do but we'd just as soon not do that this time around. When you want an ice cream cone or a cowboy suit or you want to hit the peanut butter jar a good lick, those are things I can let you do." You show the little boy or little girl that you can help them and you give them some of the things they need and that's better than nothing, a lot better than nothing. I found that buying myself a $160 horse named Whiskey was something the little boy in me desperately needed. It wasn't the sports cars and other things I had bought myself earlier that I really needed. But that horse really helped quiet down the little boy and saved me all kinds of money that I otherwise would have spent on things I didn't really want.

There are many ways of healing the subconscious. My areas of ignorance on that subject are exceptionally vast. All I can say is that I have seen this process I'm talking about have a healing effect on the subconscious. Just exactly how it works and what works, I can't tell you because I don't know exactly. But it does work, kind of, and it works better than any other system I've seen so far. And of course, the goal eventually is to unite the conscious and the subconscious mind to a substantial degree. And then we are increasingly free because we're spinning down the Mississippi River and we haven't got the feeling that fifty-six times a day we're going to have that little guy down below put us on a sandbank and have to dig our way back out. We're going down the Mississippi River figuring, "Hey, we'll probably go along most of the day and not go crazy when the little guy down below puts me up in a sandbank. And that's a real improvement over what it used to be for me."

Another good way of seeing if our subconscious is healing is to watch our dream life. When most of our bad dreams disappear, that's a sign the subconscious is getting cleared up.

SIX

Winning Freedom for Ourselves by Accepting Others

Once when I started talking about accepting others, my wife said, "Jess, one basic question I've seen people have about their relationship with others is: 'I can do what's right for me up to where it starts hurting somebody else, then I've got to stop and do what's right for the other person.'"

There are a couple of problems in there. It assumes that you're a worm, and when you do the things that are really right for you, that's going to hurt other people. That's one bad assumption. I find that until I start doing the things that are right for me, I'm not really much good to anybody. Now, yes, there are a few occasions when the things I do hurt other people around me. That's a dilemma and I don't know quite how to handle that really, but it beats the alternative. Before, when I was doing things in an attempt to please other people, I was not

141

pleasing anybody, myself or anyone else. And I was hurting everybody around me terribly most of the time.

The person in flight from themselves is of almost no use to anyone around them. They can even be a great danger both to themselves and the people around them. They are just misery and accidents waiting to happen. In attempting to avoid letting the little girl or little boy inside us out to play and avoiding the harm that might do, in some cases we ensure a far greater harm, which is to ensure that we are nothing. When I spent my time trying to impress others and please others I always failed, always, all day long.

Once I went about frying my own fish and letting the little boy or girl out to play occasionally, then I finally started being able to do the things that were right for me. I was surprised to find the people around me say that what I was doing was right for them, too. But that wasn't why I was doing it. I think where we need to get to is to see that each of us truly is a wonder. Oddly enough, that has to come slowly. I've been working on this fifteen years and I can finally glimpse off there in the future some place the fact that I'm a wonder. I can't act on that knowledge very much. If I could, I would be a different person. If I truly realized I was a wonder, I would be able to strip emotionally completely and say to you all the things I feel. But I can't do that. I can see, way off in the distance, that I am a wonder truly but I can't act on that very much yet.

Every one of the group of psychiatric nurses I spoke to had an ideal of nursing which was higher than he or she could meet. In my experience my ability to understand something always exceeds my ability to practice it. Now if I was able to see what a wonder I was then of course I would have absolutely none of the fear I have that keeps me from being more open with more people. This is the basic problem I see in our relationships with others. We have surface relationships because we don't like what we see about ourselves in deeper relationships. But that's just why we need to go into deeper relationships, so we can see ourselves more clearly.

One of the crucial needs in healing ourselves and healing the subconscious is honesty; looking at ourselves and not being alarmed. When we're alarmed we're playing God. We're saying I don't like the recipe that God used in making me. I don't mean God, religious God, I mean a higher power whom I choose to call God. We're being our own higher power. I don't want to be a sex maniac. I don't want to be a dirty slob. I don't want to be this or that. I don't want to be short, tall, fat, skinny. I don't want to be young, old, baldheaded. Whatever it is that I am, I don't want to be it.

I've never seen a person yet who didn't want to fuss around with the recipe a little bit, leave out a little of this, put in a little of that. And that's the problem. Look and not be alarmed—in the firm belief that the recipe used in making us was not only all right, it's perfection, perfection itself. Ain't I a wonder and ain't you a wonder, too. If we could come to some glimmer of that, think what we could do. We could go sallying into all kinds of places where all but angels fear to tread.

Shyness is a major problem holding us back in our relations with others, but shyness really is self-centeredness, a terrible kind of self-centeredness. People think shyness is a virtue. It isn't. Shyness is saying, I'm not good enough, they won't like me. What will people think about me? There's a terrible self-preoccupation in shyness. We're all shy because we don't like ourselves. We don't like what we do. We're positive whatever we do will be inadequate. A lot of people with attitudes like that go to church and say, "I believe." Believe what? What belief can you or I possibly have when we say, "I'm not good enough, I don't like the recipe. God must have left something out when he made me."

Also keeping us from getting close to others as near as I can see is the thing that's more hated and feared than anything else in the world—emotional intimacy. Emotional intimacy is the most awful thing you can threaten a person with. It's just like someone being with you and starting to take off all their clothes. "Do not stand emotionally naked before me. It threatens me. It frightens me for one simple reason. In emotional intimacy we see ourselves. In emotional honesty we are literally forced to see ourselves. And we don't like what we see in the mirror.

There's another problem we see in our relationships and that's our anger. On anger I've got a rule for you and it's one you're going to hate, I guarantee it. It comes from Bob Conklin, the *Adventures in Attitudes* man. Bob says, "He who angers you, conquers you." And you know what the sad news is? You and I have probably already been conquered, many times today. Who wants to be conquered? And look who we were conquered by—our enemies. They who angered us took over almost complete control of our minds and our body for a while.

I've got these funny cowboy boots and the hat to go with them. I was in the airport in Chicago, I went to that washroom and on the way there was this flannel mouth. I can spot one a mile away because I've done so much of it myself. It takes one to know one. He was talking to two young folks and he looked to me like he was about thirty-eight to forty. "Well," he says, "the way I saw the problem when I was on the national committee . . ." The self-importance and egotism just dripped. I know because

144

I've been there so often. He was just laying it on those folks and he seemed really absorbed in them. I went by about twenty feet away. When I came back he was still absorbed in that conversation. I went over and sat with Jackie and was reading the paper. They called the flight so we started wandering down the ramp and here he was again about ten feet in front of me talking to these two people. I don't know whether he knew I was back there or not but he was saying in a fairly loud voice, "Boy, I think I'll get me a Stetson and a pair of cowboy boots and really attract me some attention."

I wanted to go up and tell him, "Look, you lame-brain, you've attracted more damn attention than you can possibly know with your loud talking and slashing through life. Talk about a trout making a lot of commotion."

Then I caught myself, "Whoa there, big fella. He who angers you, conquers you. I don't want that guy to conquer me."

Out in the Crow tribe I have some good friends, the Real Birds. There is one Crow name that is really strange, White Man Owns Him. I think he was a scout for Custer. The Indians were very truthful and blunt. But I thought, I don't want that white guy that angers me to own me so I started trying to get myself unhooked from my anger.

There are a lot of people who, when I talk against anger, say, "Oh boy, Jess, anger is a good thing. And I've been taught that you've got to really let people know they're bothering you and you've got to get your anger out."

My answer to that is that's an interesting philosophy and I'm glad you've got it instead of me because I don't want it. You go ahead and you practice it and see what it's going to get you. I've seen people practice that philosophy and I don't see that it gets them many good things.

I believe in a different philosophy. That is that most of my anger comes out of my fear and my frustration, and wherever my anger comes from, fear or frustration, I want to get at the roots of it and cut it out of there. Because I've seen people go through life in peace. And they didn't get peaceful by venting their anger. In my experience, venting anger just gets people mad at you and then you've got more anger to deal with. And I've never seen people get rid of anger by venting it.

I've heard all the psychological theories on how you've got to describe your feelings and own your emotions and all those other ideas. To me those theories don't work. But that's just my experience and my observation. If you want to believe differently that's beautiful. I'm happy that you've got a theory that works. But I've never been able to get those theories to work.

I'm working on a very contrary theory in my own life and it works better for me and my friends. It says get rid of your fear and your self-centeredness and your loneliness, Jess. You won't be such an ornery, cantankerous so and so. You won't be so obnoxious and hard to get along with. That has been working much better for me than those other theories did. I've finally gotten to the point where the people around me don't conquer me very often any more compared to the way they used to.

Sure I can be bad. If people set out to ring my chimes, I suspect half of them will succeed. And they'll get ahold of my serenity for a while and I'll have to struggle to get it back as quickly as I can, but that's okay.

So to me one of the crucial things about dealing with and accepting other people is for us to see the consequences of our actions clearly. I don't need to accept anyone else if I'm willing to pay the price. But that's the rub. The price of not accepting others is a lifetime of anger and self-pity and resentment where I reflect all the hurts and all the negative things somebody said about me, because I'm so touchy. It's no fun living in that kind of skin. I know because I've lived there a long time. I could tell you something somebody said that hurt my feelings ten years ago. Now isn't that beautiful?

When we consider accepting others, it gives the impression we have an alternative which is to accept other people or not. But I see clearly now that we don't have an alternative. If we don't accept other people and the things they do, it's going to eat our insides out, so we don't have an alternative really. We can die or we can accept other people. What kind of alternative is that?

That's just like they told my friend, Vince. They said, "Vince, you've got emphysema so bad that you've got two choices: You can stop smoking or you can stop breathing." Vince said, "Let me think about that awhile." He had alternatives. He had two choices. Same for us. We can accept other people or we can let them kill us.

One of the life styles offered us in the great cafeteria of life I forgot to tell you about. There is a life style where the price tag is a long and happy life. Now do you want to know what one of the crucial descriptions of this life style is instead of those withdrawn, inhibited, or angry life styles I told you about earlier? People with this particular life style are creative, outgoing personalities with a strong sense of their mutual dependence on other people. That is a rough description of the life style of the person that tends to live a long time without hardly any illnesses because most illnesses start in the mind, even those that end up in the body.

If we won't accept other people, not only does the

147

consequence of not accepting them kill us, it alienates us from the very people we need to save our lives. That's why you are so important to me. And that's why I would hope that I would avoid deliberately offending you in the course of our time together. I would like to see as many of you as is fitting who would be interested in taking a hand in helping save my life because it's a big job and I need all the help I can get from those of you who see that we fit well together.

I recognize the mutual dependence that I have on you. I often don't understand just how and why that mutual dependence works, but I know it's important so I just accept it.

Now I don't know which of you are going to participate in saving my life. I know from experience though that some of you will play a crucial part in my life. Nancy Whitacre was in the group of nurses I spoke to. She and a secretary named Mary were the ones who read my first book and asked me to give a seminar for the psychiatric nurses and out of that came my second seminar with them, which is this book. The whole thing went so smoothly because of the early initiative of a couple of lovely people.

These are the kind of things I see happening to me. Now I didn't need everybody in that large group of psychiatric nurses to respond. I couldn't handle it if all my readers chose to say, "Jess, you're the greatest." It doesn't work that way, though. I'm such a strange nut that I suspect the more you get to know me, the less and less there are who would really want to be around me very much. For most of you, you can learn from me but you see that we aren't for each other, and that's beautiful. Because I don't need everybody. I just need a few people who really fit well with me to make a tremendous difference in my life.

I am trying to speak as straight and clear as I possibly can so that those of you who respond to me can know what it is you're responding to. I want you to know just exactly what I am and what I'm not. I'm trying not to sail under false colors. I don't want to mislead anybody.

I don't want to pretend I'm something I'm not. If I did I might chase away someone who likes me for the way I am.

This is why an accurate sense of who I am so I can communicate that to you is so important to me. And this is why it is so crucial that I learn to accept the people around me so they are free to play a part in my life if they choose, without putting up walls against them.

When I first started teaching the acceptance of others, my students would often say, "Okay, Jess, I've got to accept them but I don't have to approve of them." I realize now that is a wrong teaching. It didn't work well for anyone I knew. But a lot of people taught that. And I didn't know a good answer to it. But I know a good answer to it now.

When it comes to whether I should approve of you, my old friend said, "You don't have any business in that game, Jess. Who appointed you moral judge of the universe?" Well, nobody. Fine, then I've got no business approving or disapproving of other people.

People can come back with: "Jess? Sure, I can accept him. I can approve of him. But I don't need to approve of his actions." If you feel that then you're right back in the moral judgment business playing God. I've got enough trouble seeing what I need to do. I've got enough trouble walking through the fog. I don't have the spare time to make a lot of quick snap moral judgments about you and

149

what you might be doing. I'd best keep my nose out of your business if I value my own life.

I've got all I can do to keep on my own path in this fog, snow, and blizzard. To presume that I've got things so beautifully under control that I've got lots of spare time and energy to make moral judgments still evades the central question: Who appointed me moral judge of the universe? I can't judge anyone because I don't know the situation, the circumstances, or anything about them. In my experience, I've come to see I can't even judge myself. All I can figure out is what's best for me by the weak and faltering light of the spirit that guides each one of my steps. I don't know whether I did right or wrong in any specific case. All I can judge was whether I did the best I could do considering the special circumstances.

I may feel inside, "There was a part of that last deal that didn't turn out too well and those bad results make me wonder if that was the best I could do and maybe if I would have done it a little different it would have worked out better." Now that's not what I mean by judgment. It may sound like judgment but it isn't in the sense I'm talking about it. What I mean by judgment is the "You go to hell, I go to heaven. You're wrong. I'm right."

I see that I must seek truth. I'm looking for what's best for me as near as I can see it. If I condemn you or if I condemn myself, I condemn an innocent man. I must not judge. I seek the truth for me and I seek the courage, I seek the power, to do it.

When I succeed in angering you I take control of you. And you give up control of yourself. Do you like that? No way. You don't want me pulling your strings. And I hope to God I handle myself so you aren't pulling my strings. That's a luxury I can't afford any more. I don't want to give up control of my life into another person's hands. It's bad enough with that little guy downstairs taking over control of the machinery every once in a while. But in addition to that, to give up control into the other person's hands really hurts.

What do I do about all the people I have trouble with? Boy, I tell you I struggle. I was a teacher and I was raising hell with my students by dumping a lot of stuff on them that was really pretty hard. I was asking them to shape up and I created a lot of problems for them. So a lot of them started creating a few problems back for me.

Pretty soon I got mad at my students ahead of time. I'd walk into a new class and on the first day I'd already be half mad at them for what I knew they were going to do to me. Pretty soon I got mad at students on the campus who weren't even in my classes because I felt I just knew what kind of people they were. That was one of the reasons it got so bad I had to take a couple of years off from teaching. I walked into class the first day of the fall quarter and I was chewing my students out for all the things they were going to do to me ahead of time. I saw I didn't belong in that classroom. I went in and told my boss, "I can't take it. I've been in class for one hour and it's too long." He nearly dropped his teeth.

I stayed out for two years. For those next couple of years, most times when I would see a student walking on campus I could feel that I was still mad at him. I finally came up with a line that I said to myself when I would look at someone and have those bad feelings. "May that person be as happy right now as I someday hope to be." It was kind of a prayer for them but it was really a reminder for me. But I've seen that any time I pray for someone in the sense of asking for the best for them, it takes some of the anger out of me.

We've got all kinds of people in our lives where we just

know that acceptance of other people doesn't apply. For example, we may claim we've got the most narrow-minded, hardest-to-get-along-with boss in the world. We just know acceptance doesn't have to go that far. We can get mad at him as often as we want. My answer is, "Yes, we can, if we want to be controlled by him as often as he makes us mad." We claim to have some of the lousiest, rottenest fellow workers that the world has ever seen who, we're sure, lie awake nights thinking of insults they can heap upon our tender little bodies. They seem to know every sensitive spot we've got and they press those hot buttons of ours so easily.

We think, "Certainly we can get mad at them." And the answer is, "Yes, we can." And we can pay the price and this whole psychology system I'm talking about is a system of paying prices. Not only are you being controlled by them so they have possession of your serenity and peace of mind, but what it does to you physically is very drastic. The stress in our society comes largely out of our anger, which I think is rooted in our loneliness, our fear, and our frustrations because we can't control people and things to make everything come out right for our self-centered self.

These folks who live in good health to 120 in some of these out of the way places in the world, they're still working fairly hard at those advanced ages. Work never hurt anybody. Work isn't stress. What is done with pain is stress whether it's work or play, or nothing. And I'll tell you, being angry at somebody or letting them be angry at you and willingly participating, that's stress, that's pain. It makes you old before your time. It kills you. It makes you sick, physically as well as emotionally. That's the price tag of being angry.

I found some other ways to help me with my anger until I can get to the point where people around me don't bother me. Until then I need a stop-gap way to handle the anger. Not too long ago I came to see that each person is perfectly human. So then I said, "There is a perfect human being—they are perfectly human." At about this time, my friend Wally from Three Forks told me of his idea. He wanted the privilege for himself of being wrong. But he often found himself disliking what a person was doing. He reminded himself that that other person, as much as himself, had a right to be wrong.

Recently I have seen a better answer to the problem. I see now that one of the deepest ends I have and the people around me have is to feel we're right. So now I try to go through the day helping all the people around me be right. Whatever they suggest, even if it opposes me, is to help them be right by pointing out all the good points in their position. It sure makes life go smoother when I practice that. When I forget and start arguing with someone, I don't change their opinion, I just waste time and create a poor feeling.

I also need to accept others because if I don't I will never find those few people who can save my life. But I can't know ahead of time who these few people are so I can't discriminate. I need to reach out my hand with love and friendliness to as many people as I can and I need to welcome whoever comes rather than push people away and say, "Not you, but you." In that process I give you the gift of myself. It is the greatest gift that is mine to give. What money and physical things I have to give aren't truly mine. They are very small and inconsequential things, especially alongside the greatest gift and really the only thing that is ever really needed by someone, which is the gift of another person, the gift of ourselves.

Now other than this I don't see any other part I should

play in a person's life except not bother them and not be a problem to them. Some of the most drastic examples of this that I've ever seen are people who feel that they have to visit a dying person. But they are so obnoxious and so inappropriate there that the dying person has to rise to the heights to make an effort to make the person visiting them feel better and not be so uncomfortable and ill at ease. I'm sure many of you have seen this, someone supposedly carrying water to this dying person in an empty bucket with holes in it. They are so insensitive to the fact they bring nothing but grief and trouble.

This is an extreme example of how I owe it to another person not to bother them, not to be where I don't belong. There are two people in our town who recently had brain tumors, a man and a woman. The woman was the wife of an internist who took care of me for years. I knew her casually, both as his wife and a woman who worked in a shop run by a friend of mine. But I didn't go to see her. She and I didn't fit so there was nothing I could bring her. The man had owned a ski shop and I had done some business with him, some dealing and some trading. We'd had many good laughs together. And I have gone to see him. And as near as I can see, he was interested in seeing me and he liked to have me come back. So I went back a number of times. I was there because it seemed like a place I belonged. I was also following another basic rule of mine in that I was there because of what it did for me. I felt better if I went. But I was not going to go so I could feel better if it was going to cause him pain rather than something hopefully a little better than that.

To go back to our trout in the stream analogy, one of the biggest services a trout can render to his fellow trout is not harm them and not invade the other's territory too much. At meetings where I speak I come up to people but I am always watching very carefully, watching their faces, their bodies, watching all the signs to see whether I belong with each person or not. And whether I belong closer or further away. I've found you can tell when you pay attention. When you've got your head halfway clear you can tell better. And the more you work at it the better you can tell.

It's like the Bob Dylan song which says that you should never be where you don't belong. What had happened to a guy in this song was kind of humorous. I forget whether it was Frankie Lee or Judas Priest, but he was running down the street. It's hard to figure out a Dylan song because they're so full of fantastic images, but anyway, the guy came to this house and it had four and twenty windows and a woman's face in every one. He went running into the house and then later they carried him out on a slab. As he was being carried out a little kid was singing that the moral was that you should never be where you don't belong.

There is another argument you might be making against accepting others. You might think, "I don't have to really like that person I'm near, I'll just pretend I like him. I'll just pretend that I'm accepting him. You're asking too much of me, Jess."

Do you think you can get away with that? The answer is no. You can't. You know why? It's because each of us knows everything that everybody around us is thinking all the time. We can't always put a finger on it for sure, but we know.

Stephen, the spiritual teacher at The Farm, a commune down in Tennessee, teaches that we're all telepathic, we all know what each other is thinking. I think it's a true teaching. He says, "Everyone knows what's going on all the time. And on The Farm, we have an agreement to

155

work that out together." It's a commune with about eight hundred people, five hundred adults and three hundred kids. They've got a deal. If something is wrong between them, they work it out. Someone may argue there's nothing wrong. "Oh no, I love you, brother, really, you're just a groovy guy."

"No, something's wrong between us. Let's work it out."

Now this can't be done with just anybody on the street. The people at The Farm have made an agreement as part of being there that they will work things out. I can't do that to one of you and say, "Something is wrong between us. Let's work it out." We don't have that agreement so I don't have that right.

But this is a good example of how we can't kid ourselves thinking we're putting something over on someone, that we're fooling them. Everybody knows what's going on with everybody and how specifically we can put a finger on it varies a lot with us and our awareness and what have you. But everybody has got some dim comprehension, some uneasiness, an awareness when things aren't right, when something's going on.

I made the mistake of refusing to accept other people a lot. I'm still making it a lot. I had to make it over and over and over again until I got sick to the guts of the consequences, of the cost of my mistakes. So I feel very, very strongly about this. It's just like the guy who's rammed his head against the concrete wall 10,000 times. You ask him, "Is it fun to bang your head against the concrete wall?" "No, not at all," he says. Okay, that's the situation I'm in.

"Are we being true to ourselves if we don't at least share with the other persons what's happening, that we are angry?"

The answer there is, if you are very brave, you can do

that. What I do in that situation is I tell one of my five friends. I share with them how angry I am with some other person because so far I'm incapable of doing the thing you speak of. And then I work at getting at the roots of that anger. Where is it coming from? Is it fear? Is it loneliness? Is it needing love? Is it my frustration at not getting my way? And I work at getting rid of those things that cause the anger. Because what I've seen is that most of the people in AA used to fight anyone at the drop of a hat. They've gone from that to where most of them are very quiet and gentle people. Yet, they never vented any of their anger. They never used any of the conventional psychological systems of getting rid of anger. And they changed from the angriest people to peaceable ones. When they were drinking it took five policemen apiece to keep the peace. Yet when the big AA convention came to Denver, crime dropped way down and there wasn't hardly a policeman on the street and here were 50,000 AA's.

Now where did the miraculous change come from and how did it come about? I want to know because I'm an angry, cantankerous, hard-to-get-along-with person. But I have never really been able to share my anger with someone except maybe a long time later. Now, I'm a hard case. I'm a very difficult person. I would never presume that you would have this same degree of difficulty.

"I can buy that we're not supposed to show our anger, but how we keep from getting angry inside?"

I used to think my anger came out of my fear. I see now that it mostly comes out of my selfishness, my self-centeredness. I want things my way. I want people to act the way I expect or hope they will act. When they don't I get frustrated and angry. When I have a few people who I know will treat me well, it helps me from wanting everybody to treat me my way. That's where my five friends come in. They have helped make me quieter and more peaceful.

"But anger seems so spontaneous. What if you don't have those five friends around you all the time?"

In my experience, anger just seems like it is spontaneous, but it isn't. As I've got five people a day who love me, I'm not popping off as much as I used to. So anger isn't as spontaneous as I thought it was. The more and deeper an awareness we have of our feelings, the more we can see ourselves getting ready to pop off and just looking for an excuse.

"I would love not getting angry, but what I know about feelings is that they don't respond to orders. I can't tell myself don't be angry. So what do you do?"

What I do is I go tell my friend how angry I was at another person and we can laugh about it. That way I get rid of the anger in a way that isn't going to make it any worse. Any way I've seen of saying my anger to that other person makes it worse. That works for me, I'm not saying what's for you. Another thing I do is I'm doing my homework ahead of time by having loving encounters during the day. So now I don't have to watch myself getting angry inside near as often as I used to. This is what I'm doing about my anger at students. Most of that has gone away now.

"Isn't a lot of anger displaced? I would think a lot of what we call spontaneous anger is displaced."

Sure. You look back in the day and you see what you were really burned at is something that happened earlier rather than at the later moment that set you off. When you can track your anger back to see what really set it off, then that helps, too. I find much of my anger that was directed at our chidren was because I was mad at somebody bigger, but was afraid of being angry at that person so I got angry at somebody little like my kids. See how harmful that is to people near me, as well as myself?

"It seems to me that if you want to avoid getting angry you have to give up trying to run things and control everything. Then the other person isn't stepping on your toes, toes that nobody ought to come close to."

Right. The root of anger is our self-centeredness. When people don't do what we want, then we get frustrated.

"I'm in a situation where two fellow faculty members are hurting each other. One is really suffering. It bothers me not to do anything about it."

Okay. I'm not talking about not doing anything about it. I'm talking about not getting angry.

"Well, is it anger or is it just there, if it bothers you?"

Well, I try to do what I can about the situation, seeking to have the same calm spirit that I have as I go about turning the lights on in my office or putting stamps on my letters. Now if I don't work on the problem in that spirit then it is very easy to become part of the problem instead of part of the solution. And I've got enough problems without becoming part of new ones. Now even if I can't act in that calm spirit, I will act in the best spirit I can if the matter is so drastic it outweighs the price I'm going to pay.

"But isn't it true that anger turned inward often ends up in multiple psychosomatic complaints?"

Yes, if you don't do something about that anger, but we're not talking about not doing something about it. We're talking about doing a lot of things about it.

"I'm wondering how acceptance of others and anger relates; do they have any relation to one another?"

A lot of anger we have at other people comes from their behavior to us, which is produced previously by our lack of acceptance of them, which they feel. If I come into a situation bristling, touchy, self-centered, I'm going to disturb people. It's in the air waves, it's in the vibrations. And they'll do some things they wouldn't otherwise. I see it in my horses. I had some horses in the corral and was going to let my friend, Dick, who was new to horses ride this one horse. He got on the horse and the horse threw a fit. I got my friend off as quick as I could. I thought, "What happened to my horse? Is there a cocklebur under the saddle?" I went and looked. The horse had a lot of life but I had never seen him act that way before. So my friend held the bridle for me and I got on my horse and he was just fine. So I told Dick to turn him loose and he stood just fine.

What was the problem? Dick got on that horse and he was sending him seventy-six different messages. The horse was confused and frightened. So Dick was producing the behavior that was a problem to him. Same with the lack of acceptance of people. I was producing most of the disordered behavior from the people around me that would make me get mad at them.

"I think if you're close and you have a nourishing relationship you can get insights by discussing your anger. If you and I were totally in a relationship, I would say: 'Hey, Jess, you really made me angry yesterday. Could we talk about it?' I think sometimes we can get insight into our behavior through this."

Yes. But the thing I find is that basically you and I don't have a good heart towards each other or that situation wouldn't have gone that far. What you're talking about may be possible with someone we have to be in association with, if it's not a voluntary association. In my experience, in voluntary associations, when there is the kind of difficulty you are speaking of, this is a precious sign to me. It says to me, "Hey, we've got no business with each other at all." I find in mutuality we have such good hearts towards each other almost right from the start that it's almost impossible for me to have a misunderstanding. It isn't one of a thousand transactions between my friends and I where there will be a misunderstanding.

"A lot of times I agree with you. A lot of times it's your own hang-up where your problem comes from."

Right. And so often, by bringing it up that way, by saying, "You made me mad," I'm implying that the other person is at fault. And I tell the other person that they are going to have to change around some.

Instead, I find I can just tell myself, "Hey, Jess, you were cranky and mad at the world," and just let it go. If it was one of my five friends, I could say, "Hey, Jerry, sometimes I sure get crabby and do some dumb things." But even that is usually unnecessary because he knew it without me saying it.

But in my experience if even one out of five thousand transactions between me and one of the five friends is of that caliber, then the minute it gets that bad to me that relationship is gone. At least the relationship is gone temporarily, because it's a sign of something a lot more drastic and a lot deeper than anything we're going to be able to patch up with a few words.

At this point my wife Jackie wanted to make a contribution. "Somebody said something about going to one of their friends and saying, 'Boy, I really got angry at you yesterday.' That has to be one of my pet hates because it's laying my trip on that other person. The fact I get angry at another person is my problem."

That's the same thing as when we go to somebody and say, "Hey, what you did made me angry." The very bad implication is, "There's something wrong with you." And there isn't anything wrong with that person. There's nothing wrong with any of my five friends. In those relationships with them, the only person I see screwing up is myself. This business of telling someone they make you mad is very fashionable. It's talked a lot in psychological circles. We're told to "Go and describe your feelings, admit it's how you feel." But I haven't seen it work very well. I haven't seen anybody become a calm and serene individual because of it. And I'm a very scientific and pragmatic person. If you say you've got a good theory, I want you to demonstrate it for me and I want you to show me the results.

"The benefit I find in owning my feelings and my anger is that it identifies to me that I am upset. If I just deny it and repress it and don't recognize it, I don't know what I'm feeling. If I do recognize it, then I can say something to the other person. It's something that I see in them that I don't like about myself. And then I recognize the feeling and I say, 'It wasn't them, it was me, I'll have to work on that.' Where if I just repress it, I hurt myself inside and I can't make any progress."

Right. I'm not arguing for repression. I'm saying that we go through this process that you speak of with some person other than the one you're angry at.

"Suppose there was a meeting and you knew there were some people in the meeting who said a lot of things you didn't agree with. Would you attend the meeting?"

Yes. This is my problem and I've got to develop a certain degree of tolerance for other people's positions. Partly I need to learn to disagree without being disagreeable. I need to learn to disagree without taking everything personally. With a group of fellow workers, there will automatically and inevitably be disagreements about policies. As long as we can keep the disagreements on the issues without getting any more personal than we can manage, things go better. But there is no such thing as an issue that isn't personal. The person who tries to say something critical and yet defend themselves by saying, "I'm not getting personal," is getting exceptionally personal right then. The person who says, "Why do you take this personally?" usually misses the feeling. There is no way I can disagree with your policy without disagreeing with you in some degree. We all have a deep feeling of wanting to be right that gets tangled up with our point.

Now the way I disagree can be more or less of a disagreement with you personally. So I would try to disagree with your point as much as I could and as little with you. But I would be a fool to say, "Let's conduct this thing on a high level and not let personalities enter into it." How can I disagree with your policy without to some degree disagreeing with you?

"If you experience anger with any one of your five friends, do you handle anger with them by going to another of the five friends and talking about it?"

I've never been angry with one of my five friends. I've been in a couple of rough situations with them where there was a momentary difficulty which would have made me plenty mad if it was someone else. But right from the beginning there was such an affinity between us that it protected us against anger. It's the same thing you see when someone does something that would usually make you mad but there is such a good feeling between the two of you that you just laugh.

"Would you say something about that in the context of marriages?"

Sure. I have two levels of mutual relationships. One level is with my family. In my wife's case I married her when she was nineteen and I was twenty-three. Now I did a very intelligent thing for all the wrong reasons. I married this gorgeous black-haired broad with all kinds of everything. And then I found what I got was a lady with a magnificent mind and a wonderful, gentle heart. I have five children and I didn't pick them out so they would be specific personalities that would groove on me. And there is a real range in the mutuality I have with those five kids. There are times with some of my kids when the biggest favor I can do them is stay out of their way. In other cases there can be tremendous mutuality. That's simply the way it is. Beautiful.

Now in those relationships, they were not entered into on the same basis as my five friends which are absolute, 100 per cent pure voluntary associations entered into in the mid-forties in age when I was looking for something very specific, faces that lit up when they saw me.

The family relationships are most crucial to me. They are the most sustaining. Next are my five friends. My first priority is to my higher power, my second is to my family, my third priority is to my five friends.

But there is a difference in those relationships because of the way they were entered into and they have a different basis. Jackie and I do disagree, sometimes violently. And we have to work out our problems along some of the lines we are talking about. "I'm mad at you for this and that reason." We're trying to do that as well as we can. But I'm not talking about the marriage relationships here, I'm talking about the principles of relating to people except the person you're married to. But it's a different principle. I have a deep commitment to my wife and children. I don't have anything approaching that degree of commitment with anyone else.

If a marriage association was entered into exactly as a mutual need relationship it would be on a purely voluntary basis with no commitment except for the mutual at-

164

traction. Jackie would bring her property in and I would bring mine. Our property would stay in separate ownerships. Half of what I earned would go to Jackie and we would split expenses and have our own savings. We would agree to live in the same house together but the minute either person wanted to split, he or she took their things and their person and went their separate way. This assumes there would be no consequences for children or anything. That would be a marriage that existed on the same basis as a mutual relationship. But most marriages weren't entered into that way and they don't have those same consequences. We happen to have five children and all kinds of things that make it different so that a permanent commitment is necessary. It's a different situation and only an idiot applies the same rules to all different situations. We're talking about guidelines, we're talking about thinking, not a slavish obedience to rules.

"Tell me about finding a friend you can trust to tell about the corks, the skeletons in your closet. Comment on how you decide who to trust with what fears."

I've got a sensitivity along that line, finally, that I've carefully cultivated. At first you open your heart to five people you think you can most open up with. On the average three of the five will respond and the other two will run for cover. Sometimes you're not as lucky as that. That's how to get better. It's just like touching. You get better by practicing. You get better by falling on your nose. How do you learn to ride a bicycle? You get on the bicycle and you fall down. And you develop a feeling for it.

I don't think a person I've opened my heart to has ever broken a confidence on me in the last three to five years. So I'm getting real good at finding intimate friends I can trust. But I've practiced.

"Will you comment on my idea? The more we are self-accepting and enjoy aloneness and handle loneliness, the better quality relationships we will develop. That way there is no desperate dependency on the other person to keep me from loneliness."

Right. Now I think it isn't so much that comes out of handling aloneness. For me, at least, it is the warm relationships that wipe out loneliness. And that makes it possible to be alone without being lonely. This is the point of having five friends. A lot of people say, "Can't I get by on just one?" And the answer is you have to start with one friend but, I don't see any way you can stop there because there comes to be a dependency. If you have just one source of supply on anything, to me you can't help but have a dependency. And a dependency in my experience is always a harmful thing. It's harmful to us and it's harmful to the person we're dependent on. It's just like the girl who came to me and said, "Jess, Jess, I've got to get Willie back."

I said, "Does Willie want to come back?"

She said, "No, but I've got to get him back."

I said, "Do you love him?"

She said, "Yeah, I love Willie."

"Well, for God's sake, then, let him go."

"But I want Willie."

She's got a dependency on Willie. And she isn't caring about what Willie wants. She's thinking about what she wants. So I find the test of a real relationship is that they are truly loving relationships, because always, in a real relationship you want the very best for that other person up to and including splitting from you.

If any of my mutual friends wants to split from me that's all right because I want what's best for them. I want what will make them happy. And again I don't have a dependency. We are dependent just like I am dependent on food or water. But that doesn't mean that if you say I can't ever have orange pop again that I'm going to die. There are a lot of other liquids I can use to meet my needs. So the key is we are all dependent on people but we don't have a dependency on a specific person.

"Isn't every deed we perform selfish and aren't you saying that we should accept that?"

Yes, selfish, but in a good way. I think we should look at our own need. I act only to meet my needs. The more I've done that, the more people tell me I'm helping them. Before, no one would ever say that about me. In the old days when I was helping people a lot, nobody ever said, "You're helping me." Now that I'm trying to avoid doing anything that isn't right for me, all kinds of people are coming to me and saying, "You're helping me, Jess."

I'm not so stupid that I can't see that there's a chance I might end up helping some of you. But why put the emphasis on that when you are giving me so much? Why should I say, "Look what I'm doing for you. I'm here with you tidying up your life, cleaning it up." But I would be ignoring that you are doing ten times that for me. You may choose to argue, "No, Jess. You're doing ten times for me what I'm doing for you." Well okay, whatever you feel. But I'm not intending to help you. I'm not trying to help you.

You see the problem is that if I say that I'm going to help you I have to presume that you need help and it's stupid for me to presume such a thing. Secondly, it presumes that I have the help that I offer. If I say, I'm going to help you and you'd like a hundred thousand dollars, I have to say, "Well, I didn't mean that." Well, just exactly what did you mean? Well about five cents' worth. Well, then why didn't you say, "I'm a big helper. I'm going to give you five cents if not too many ask." That gets my offer right down to reality.

"What do you think of Glasser's *Reality Therapy?* It seems you focus on many of the same points such as a awareness of self, setting realistic goals, making the commitments, not giving up, etc. Do you consider this a man-made philosophy?"

To me, all psychological systems have substantial elements of all the same things in them or they wouldn't work. If there are universal laws, then the systems have to have some of that lawfulness reflected in them or the system won't work. To me some psychological systems reflect more of the lawfulness that's in the universe than others. It's just like Einstein's $E = mc^2$. His theory reflected and encompassed more of the lawfulness of the universe in its one small equation than anything up to that time had. So the point is all of our systems are man-made or man-discovered, but some of them are more encompassing than others.

As I mentioned in an earlier chapter, the system I am talking about is the one I observed, as well as I could see, in twelve-step groups like Alcoholics Anonymous. To me that's where most of what I'm talking about comes from. While I talked about this point before, I need to return to it and discuss it again because of its importance. A real good way to find out how good this system I'm talking about works compared to others is to try it out, see if it works. If it works for you better than any other system then it is, for you, a better system. If it works for a whole lot of people better than someone else's system, then the system discovered by the twelve-step groups out of their necessity is an exceptionally fine system.

Almost all psychological systems ignore a higher power. To me that's a serious limitation. The weakness of most psychological systems is shown when it comes to the treatment of a tough problem—alcoholism. With this problem all of the other systems have a record of almost complete failure.

The twelve-step program of psychology that includes the higher power is able to remove the drinking behavior. It also brings about other crucial psychological changes in a high percentage of people who want to get well badly enough to give the system a try and attend meetings.

When faced with the evidence that no conventional psychological system will change the alcoholic's behavior, psychology has largely chosen to ignore the evidence that its systems are faulty. Because the twelve-step program mentions the name of God, psychologists think it is a religious system, and not a psychological system. But it is a psychological system. The twelve-step program believes that any concept of a higher power will work, from God, Allah, Buddha, the group, or the big Indian on the hill. Most Christians say that won't work and only their particular brand of Christianity will work. The only problem is that the evidence won't support them. Some people have had their alcoholism removed by their brand of Christianity. But for each of them, there are many others who have tried and failed only to have success with the twelve-step programs.

So it isn't only psychology that has failed with alcoholism. Conventional religion has failed, too. So the success of the twelve-step programs with the alcoholic presents some equally serious difficulties for the narrow religionists as well as the psychologists. And neither group has shown much interest in reexamining their prejudices and their basic propositions.

The biggest problem, I think, with the twelve-step system for most psychologists is the use of the word God.

Their prejudices against anything that smacks of religion are so strong that they don't get past the word God and see that it is used in a very special and very technical way. If they could study the system long enough and well enough, they would see that "God" means any belief in anything outside themselves such as an order in the universe. They can't be psychologists unless they believe in an order in the universe. Without such an order and lawfulness, there is no basis for any psychological generalizations. If there is no order, everything that happens is completely random and unpredictable. But if everything is random and unpredictable, then all the rules and theories could be wiped out because they are based on an observed lawfulness and order. If one dog salivates when Pavlov rang his bell when food was presented, then all dogs will salivate under the same conditions. That's the basic lawfulness that has to be demonstrated for there to be science of psychology.

So all the twelve-step program really needs from a person as a concept of a higher power is a belief in that same lawfulness that psychologists and all other scientists of necessity believe in. That can serve as an adequate god that will get you sober because it is some power higher than yourself—some power outside yourself, God as you understand him. So any psychologist almost by necessity believes in a higher power in the special sense it is used in the twelve-step programs.

Arising out of the higher power problem, there seems to me to be one other serious problem psychology systems have. As near as I can see, most systems try to get a person to turn inward and become more inner-directed and less directed by the pull of environment and old memories. But, as I mentioned earlier, it seems to me that each person has basically two inner voices they have to choose between. One inner voice is very self-centered but very shortsighted and that shortsightedness hurts the total self. The other inner voice is higher power—centered and not shortsighted so it has the best sense of what is, in the long run, in the truer interest of the self. But since I find the true self is in harmony with the other true selves around us, what looks selfish really isn't. It not only puts us in harmony with our self and the higher power but also the people around us.

By failing to point out what I believe is the distinction between these two voices and by not giving people a method of distinguishing the two voices, most people are left by the psychological systems as deeply locked up in self as when they started. I think this is why many people are so critical of the self-development movements. Many critics see people go into self-development programs like encounter, EST, Yoga, or what have you and end up even more locked up in self than when they started. I think there are real excesses in the self-help movement that increase "me-ism." But, to me, any excesses or mistakes are almost inevitable as a rank materialist such as myself tries to turn inward and find the true self. Another major criticism of the self-help movement is that the people in it lose all their political activism. I think that charge is largely unwarranted because I think all is changed is the arena where the activity is. I see people as they become more enlightened as being more active in quiet ways that don't attract as much attention but where a lot more is accomplished.

I think where each of us must start is to see that we can't do anything about accepting others until we come to grips with our self. But I think relationships with others is where it really starts for us. You can't find anyone who's living their life in real freedom who isn't able to live in relationship with people in some good way. So if I had to pick a place to start living a freer life, I'd say get into relationships with others and learn as you go. When we spend all our time working on the self so we can get ready to get into relationships with others, it's easy to lie to ourselves about how good we are doing. It's only when we really get into relationships with others and are willing to face the truth we see about ourselves, that we are forced to see our strengths and weaknesses in that relationship. So we get truth, fast. And we get the beautiful, loving support that only another loving human being can give us. And that changes most everything.

SEVEN

This Lovely Society We Have Worked Out for Ourselves

I want to talk to you about acceptance of our society. You see, before, when I had no sense of a higher power, there was no way I could accept the things that happened in society. All around me was death and destruction. I saw the death and destruction as the work of a god and a terrible immorality. "What kind of god would do this or allow this?" was my cry. I see now my focusing on the death and destruction in society was my attempt to distract myself from the real immorality which was me not being honest and open with myself and giving of myself or in harmony with myself. That's the only immorality I know about any more. It's the only thing I can really do anything about and it's the only thing I'm responsible for. As to whether you choose to give of yourself or not, that's your business, not my business.

But when I didn't have any higher power, when I was

my own god, then nothing that happened in the world made any sense. Most everything was bad: starvation, suffering, crime, poverty, and most of all, death. But I finally came to see, as I do now, that none of these things I feared were bad. It looks to me that even death is simply the start of a new growth program or the granting of a deep peace and relief. Two years ago Elisabeth Kübler-Ross told me of her findings on the peace felt by people who died briefly and were brought back to life. Working completely independently of her, Moody, in his great book *Life After Life,* found the same things she had found. More and more I see that all suffering is temporary. All the things I feared and worried about were largely material. And I came to see that there was a higher power and that getting in harmony with that power was restorative.

For example, here's an alcoholic who is forty-five years old. He comes crawling in on his hands and knees up the steps to a second-floor AA meeting with shoes that don't match. You can imagine the state of his whole body, practically destroyed physically. Here he is now, seventy-two years old and he is more vigorous and healthy than he was by far when he was forty-five. To me that's a redemptive system where we're given back physical, mental, and spiritual things we thought we'd lost forever.

You take a liver as bad as his liver must have been, and you would have imagined it damaged beyond repair. But it's just like when you quit smoking, your lungs restore themselves. There is a restorative process in the body and the mind once you get it working for you. You heal. You grow back. Once you see that process at work, you know there is almost nothing that is irreversible. There is very little damage and destruction that is permanent. The stuff that is permanent and lifelong we see can be borne. We've all seen people with equal handicaps. In one case the handicap destroys the mind and in the other case the handicap is transcended and literally opens the door to life itself. Helen Keller, born blind and deaf, transcended her handicap and ended up thanking God for her body, which, in her hands, became a beautiful instrument to make contact with the world.

So with this new perspective it is now possible for me to have some understanding of enough things in society so that I can accept the things that I see in the world. Like over there in the Sahara, there is a whole bunch of people who are starving to death because the weather has literally changed and overgrazing has increased the size of the desert. The rain belt changed because our earth, as always, is in the process of weather changes. So the Sahara moved south a hundred or two hundred miles and of course wiped out a whole area that was previously agricultural. The people who were there aren't just going to evaporate from the face of the earth or move south two hundred miles. The land to the south is already occupied. So a lot of these folks died and more of them will die.

I don't say that I can understand all this. But I've got enough of an understanding of it and enough realization and knowledge that it's not my business to necessarily know all the answers to everything. So the problem is a simpler problem for me now. I don't mean to minimize the seriousness or consequences of the problem. But for me it is a very simple problem. I must sit down and decide what specific things I am going to do about the starvation in the south Sahara. Many people hear me talk this way and they think I mean apathy instead of acceptance. They think I mean doing nothing about a problem. I don't mean that. If someone is so concerned about that starvation that they move to the south Sahara, that's beautiful. But where people get in trouble, I see, is in their lack of acceptance of the problem. It exists. They want to condemn the suffering and do nothing about it. They don't want to move to the south Sahara because if they did, who would also worry about the starvation in India? So am I going to go to the south Sahara and do what I can? Am I going to send food? Am I going to write to my congressman and say, "I want you to do what you can to get food over there?" I must simply do whatever specific things I can.

Now in the old days I would have spent a lot of time thinking about the injustices of it. I would have gone around looking worried. Now, boy, that's a beauty, I tell you. I'm thinking about that problem. But what was I doing all the time I was thinking about that problem? I was stone-blind to some honest-to-god problems right around me that had been given to me and me alone.

I would never have been invited to come speak to a group like my psychiatric nurses because no group with any wisdom would have asked me to come. In the old days I'd give speeches in Toastmasters about "Dedication to Excellence" and I was so blind I couldn't see my whole life was a contradiction to my title. People would fall asleep because those speeches were the dumbest thing you could ever imagine. Why? Because I never had but half my wits about me. The other half was always thinking about problems far away that I wasn't ever going to do anything about. But, boy, don't you try to call me on it. "I'm an informed, concerned citizen. I'm thinking about that problem. Only through constructive thinking about it can something positive ever happen about that problem. "But if you tried to pin me down on just exactly what I was going to do and when I was going to do it, I'd get mad at you. I'd call you all kinds of names. "You are sure a cold, hardhearted person. You don't have any feelings and sensitivity for people like I do. Can't you see how aware and concerned I am. Can't you see the frown on my forehead?" Oh, I'd get real irate.

There wasn't a contemporary problem in America I wasn't thinking about. I know because I took special magazines like *New Republic* to tell me about problems I wouldn't hear about otherwise. Yet, in my own personal life there wasn't hardly any problem that I would have been able to do something about that I was working on. Why wasn't I working on my own problems? I was so busy kidding myself into believing I was thinking a lot about these world problems that I'd talk about any one of them at the drop of a hat. Yet there was no way I would talk any about my own narcissism and my self-preoccupation.

I watched a farmer I know spend so much time helping his neighbors that he lost his own farm. Isn't that a beautiful message to send to your wife and children? The family soon broke up and went to the winds.

Through the process of a long and glorious life of making mistakes, I've come to the position where I am more ready to work on the problems that are given to me. I used to try to eat the elephant, the whole elephant at once. My problems come to me now one at a time all lined up in little bite-sized pieces. Where do you start? It doesn't matter.

How is life presented to me? Five minutes at a time. If I have on my mind, "How can I write a good book for you someday?" Or, "How can I write some good pages for you tomorrow?" I don't ever succeed very well. But if I keep my attention on the next five minutes, I've got a chance of succeeding with these pages. If I put a bunch of those five minutes together, where in most of them I succeeded in paying attention to what I was doing, lo and behold, the pages I come to tomorrow can succeed, too.

In my egocentric, self-preoccupied role I spent a lot of time worrying about the world. "Why did that sniper shoot all those people? How did it feel for them to die? Isn't it terrible? What's the younger generation coming to? Why can't they be good people like me?" Like me? Why can't they be like me and kill the people right next to them in their neglect and ignorance of those folks' problems?

This is why I've come to see I need to get out of the god business. This is why I've come to see that society is part of a beautiful harmonic system, part of this gigantic cafeteria I mentioned earlier where folks are stepping up and getting a good, big helping of just what they want in an awful lot of cases. And the things that I thought were the real problems in this world were material problems always. And I was the worst of the materialists. I thought real problems were all the material problems: food, shelter, clothing.

I find now, in my experience, there is only one problem and each of us has a precious opportunity to solve that problem, hopefully as undisturbed by the people around them as possible.

To me that one simple problem is: Are we going to live completely wrapped up in self and the emotional sickness that comes out of it? Are we going to live caught up in self and its accompanying sickness of the mind and all of the terrible things that kind of life produces whether material prosperity, which can be terrible, or tremendous poverty, which can be equally terrible? Are we going to keep on living in sickness of the mind and worshiping self? Or, are we going to get out of the center and get in harmony with life? To me that's the only question I see in life: Which of those two ways am I going to live? We've got the precious right to live in self as long as we want. We have the precious right to suffer the consequences as long as we want. We've got the precious right to inflict the consequences of that choice on the people around us as long as we want. Here again, if we're going to live that way, we just have to be willing to accept the consequences of inflicting that punishment.

I'll fight for the right that each of you have to do what you most believe in for you up to the point where the law says, "No." If anybody is trying to murder somebody else, I'll do whatever I can to stop them. I'll throw a chair at them or something so they don't murder someone else. But if somebody is cutting someone else down I can't go throw a chair at them because then it's me who is breaking the law and they can have me thrown in jail.

In my view the second crime, that of cutting someone down, is just as bad as the first. But there the law isn't on my side. And I can't break the law to do what looks to me might be wrong unless I'm very certain that I can improve things and unless I'm willing to pay the price for breaking the law.

So I let society go its way with the one qualification that I will do what I can on those things that I see it is my place to do. Now, oddly enough, I'm doing lots more for society than I used to do and yet I'm not trying to and I'm not spending near as much time on it. But I'm doing a lot more things productively outside my five friends.

I see now very clearly that the problems I had accepting society were because things didn't work out the way I wanted them to. How did I want society run? I didn't want any death, sickness, or suffering. But how can we learn unless we suffer the pain of touching the hot stove? And I didn't want anyone to be deprived of any material want. I was the crassest of materialists and I didn't see that the biggest problem both the rich and the poor have is trying to live out of harmony with the spiritual side. You can give a poor man lots of money and find he still has most of his pain. How can that be? For the same reason that the rich men of the country have so much pain and misery. The material side of life is only one of three sides. There's the mental side which needs development, too. But most important there's the spiritual side that is the center of life. And that's the side of us that's usually least developed so we are out of harmony with it. And it's the side of us that gives us the most pain as we ignore our spiritual quest, live out of harmony with our spiritual dimension, and live a self-centered life. But I couldn't understand that idea in my earlier days. I had my church and yet I was an all-out materialist. There was so little understanding of the spiritual side of life in me. So all my objections were to the physical, material problems in the world.

We don't need to go to Africa or Guatemala to find suffering. The people right around you and me are suffering so bad they are killing themselves in the night because they feel so alone, they feel no one cares about them. And the sadness is, they are the ones close to us. They are the ones life has placed us closest to and by that means life has indicated that we are the ones most likely to play a part in each other's lives. A friend of mine woke up one morning and found his buddy had cut his throat with a paring knife during the night because his emotional pain was so bad.

How can I relieve suffering in Africa if I can't relieve suffering in my friend? Or in my family? How can I be so arrogant to think that I'm the only one who sees the problem in Africa? There are three billion people on this earth. How can I feel that I must lead the way in pointing out the world's problems or everyone else will miss them? And most crucially, what about the people around me? I'll never forget watching my "internationalist" friends and their concern for the world's problems because in the midst of our concern I can see now we were doing hurtful things to one another.

I have come to see that we have no choice but to get in harmony with all of the society except that little part we've been given to change. I grant you, we can choose not to get in harmony with society but the price of living out of harmony is so painful that once we see the price, it isn't a very pleasant choice. It's like our freedom to steal. We can be a criminal and steal and spend most of our life in prison or worrying about going to prison. But the price for stealing is so high that it would never make sense to make such a choice.

Then why would the criminal steal? The social determinists say it's because of his environment or his poverty. "Poor baby, he can't help it." But that argument has some serious weaknesses. Most of his brothers and sisters don't steal and they had the same environment, so that can't be all the answer. Most people with as much poverty don't steal, so that can't be all the answer. Also, white collar crime, stealing by people who aren't in poverty, is probably a much bigger item by far. So where does the answer lie?

I think the reason a person steals is to create a disturbance in his life that's so demanding of his time and attention that it will take his mind off his emotional problems. We see the clearest example of this in the compulsive gambler. I could never understand compulsive gambling until I found that the only time a gambler has a real problem is when he wins. He thinks he wants to win. But

181

when he does win, he all of a sudden loses most of the things gambling does for him, which is his intense preoccupation in the gamble. Will he win? If he loses, how can he pay his debts? The minute he wins, his problems and preoccupations are momentarily lifted. He has won, he has money, he can pay his bills. But he needs a big bet to be preoccupied with. The only way he can solve his problem is to put a new, bigger, riskier bet down so he can be preoccupied again. It's just like getting drunk. The big bet or the bottle takes your mind off your emotional pain.

Where does the emotional pain come from? Again, it doesn't come from environment or poverty because it exists in all environments and among the rich and the poor. The emotional pain comes from living the self-centered life. The little child lying on the floor screaming and kicking his heels is like us. He is having emotional pain because life won't hand him the candy bar he wants. But when he grows up, rather than get in harmony with life and get rid of his emotional pain, he throws a temper tantrum and will go get drunk to ease the pain.

And it's right here that I see where the problems of society come from. And all the structures I used to condemn in society are systems I now see are designed and used by people like you and me to ease our emotional pain. Those structures serve the same purpose as an anesthetic in an operation. With anesthesia there is still pain, but no awareness of the pain at the conscious level. Our body feels the pain. We sure know we had pain when we come out of surgery. But we didn't feel the pain at the time. So all the structures in society I condemned were the things other people were using to anesthetize themselves. And, of course, even more troubling were the consequences of those structures.

What are some of the structures we use to anesthetize ourselves? As I see it, the list includes most of what we think is society, but only the part of a structure that provides us an intense and prolonged preoccupation is an anesthetic. For example, alcohol is a beautiful thing when it's a friendly beer between friends or a glass of wine with a meal. But for some it's carried way past that to where it numbs the mind. Same with all other things that can numb the mind where there is an extreme preoccupation with them. Games, sports, travel, intellectual pursuits, social position, revolutionary movements, religion, bureaucracies, organizations, sex, work, etc.

Let's look at alcohol as an example. If no one ever drank more than a couple of social drinks, alcohol would be no more of a problem in our society than water. But some people need alcohol to numb their pain. Too many drinks don't do anything for me. They put me to sleep. But for my alcoholic friends, drink does the opposite. It sends them off into the land where the impossible dreams all come true and they are giants striding the earth and everything is possible for them.

But gradually it takes more and more alcohol to give the same effect. And there are some terrible side effects. The drinking uses up so much money that it creates instant poverty. Part of this is our fault because we have taxed alcohol so heavily that it is three or four times as expensive to drink as it would be without the tax. Even worse than the poverty is the blindness to life from alcohol. In the drunken blindness of alcohol, wives and children suffer grievously from terrible physical and emotional beatings. Some girls are even the victims of incest. I've had some girls admit this but I've never heard of a father admitting it.

There's another terrible damage from alcohol and that's

183

in car accidents. Half the people who are killed each year are killed because of drinking, usually someone else's drinking. When an alcoholic smashes into another car and kills the father and one son, the mother and the other son have a life of suffering ahead. Multiply these consequences by the six to ten million alcoholics in the country and you see what just one escape, that of alcohol, costs us. But there are lots of other escapes that are even more common and wide ranging in their effects on society than alcohol.

So these are the prices our society pays for just one kind of escape from emotional pain. And the effects from just this one pebble thrown in the stream of life send ripples out in all directions as consequences which cause new consequences.

We could solve many of these problems if we wanted to, but we don't want to that bad. We could pass a law that the first driving-while-drinking offense would cost us our driver's license for a year and a second offense would send us to prison for a year. Such a law would cut deaths drastically and improve the taxi business. But we have a mutual agreement in society not to take another person's sick game away as long as he doesn't mess with ours. So it's easier to understand society when we see it as a plan worked out and agreed to by most all of us to numb ourselves against pain.

My own case is very instructive because the escapes I used to numb my pain are so much more common. The most important of my intense preoccupations was to impress other people. I was constantly looking for the clothes, cars, guns, clubs, activities, and other things that would impress other people. Money was no object when a new suit or a new car was needed. And I could come up with a thousand reasons other than the real one for why I needed what I wanted to have. And, of course, that's a great way to create instant poverty at a fairly high level.

I also used my work to run away from life. I would bring work home so I didn't need to be a father or husband. I was too tired. And when work wasn't enough to hide a flare-up of emotional pain, I would create a crisis in my work. I would put off some important job until it created a whole lot of new problems along with the job itself. By the time I had done the job plus put out all the extra bonfires I had created, a new crisis would be built up. So I was able to go from crisis to crisis completely preoccupied in my work. All the while I was justifying what I was doing as being for the good of my family.

Now isn't that a lovely way to live? And like the alcoholic, look at the damage I did to the other people around me. There is no way I can go back and live my early years over again with my wife and my children. I told them by my actions that they were not as important as my work. The only thing that was important was me keeping my head buried in my navel. As I have come to realize these things now my kids are all pretty well grown and all I can do is just live today with them and Jackie as well as I can. But that's a lot and it's much better than being dead from my heart attack. I was luckier than most because I got a second chance. So these are the problems in life I created for my family and all the people around me through my self-centered life.

How are other things in life corrupted by our need to escape? Sports and games are fine. I love them. They used to be compulsions for me but I now go fishing when it's a good thing for all concerned. Opening days of hunting seasons I have spent at home because something more important was happening.

Travel looks like a good thing. But it isn't when we

race two thousand miles across the country as fast as we can, race around when we get there, and race home. That's an escape.

Intellectual pursuits are one of the most beautiful things there are, but when we put our life completely into the intellect it becomes a cold and terrible force.

Social position has been some people's birthright and there's no harm in it. But when people start frantically scheming how they can climb a step on the social ladder, then that's an escape. As one old-time humorist described a certain woman's goal, "She was going to break into society if she had to use an ax."

Revolutionary movements have brought great good to us. The American Revolution gave us our freedom. Ghandi's movement gave India her freedom. The two women's movements of the early 1900s and the present day have won important rights. But a movement's goals can be twisted and used as an escape and a means of anger against each other and a way to numb personal emotional pain. I have never seen anything so good that it couldn't be perverted.

Religion is a good example. Here is the highest calling women and men can have. Yet religion can have the spirit taken out of it by turning it into a dead system of rules that obsesses the person through the day as they look for evil in the lives of others.

Bureaucracy is a good thing at its best. It's what makes our governments, institutions, and businesses go. But when we take all the personality of the individual out of consideration and ask that people be like interchangeable parts in a machine, then we lose so much in the process of creating hideouts for ourselves.

Our volunteer organizations are a peculiar feature of American life. The organizations we have built do great things. But when I have an organizational meeting every night of the month something has gone terribly wrong.

Last of the perversions is sex. In the sexual act, we see that our complete personality can come into play. Of all the mirrors of ourselves, none is more revealing than making love because here we get to see completely and accurately just what we are. But, I think, this is why sex is the most twisted of all the natural functions of man such as work, religion, and play. Sex is too revealing and we can't stand what we see. But sex, because of its overwhelming power, is easily and quickly perverted. So the feeling is unhooked from sex and it is just an act in which we aren't completely involved so we end up as spectator at our own act.

Here we see how anything in life no matter how important or how trivial can be perverted and turned into an obsession that serves the ego by numbing the pain. Each of these perversions of the life force has terrible consequences for others as well as ourselves. Add up all these terrible consequences from preventing all the things I mentioned along with the consequences that come from the consequences and it is very easy to see why there is so much pain in society.

We can pretty well show how simple this is if we would imagine that each and every alcoholic in America had a spiritual awakening right this minute such as those who are in AA have had, and stopped drinking.

It's estimated there are six to ten million alcoholics. Look at the consequences for them, their families, their jobs, and the highway accident problem. One year from now 25,000 people would be spared death and its consequences for their families and 100,000 or so people wouldn't be hurt or crippled. Think of the happy families, more productive work and community lives.

Then go back through my list and take the obsessive part away from each of the activities. See what the total impact would be. To me that clearly shows me that society isn't the problem. Society is just a reflection of our combined spiritual awareness. To change society's spiritual awareness I need to do something about my own. And the minute I do that my life begins to clear up. I see that everyone else doesn't need to change for my life to change. And then I see that as my life changes, I make it easier for other people's lives to change. I can reach out my hand, finally, with a little love and friendliness and try to awaken some poor soul. But while I can reach out, his spiritual awakening can only be between him and his higher power. I'm not in charge of spiritual awakenings.

I have come to see that this environment we have been provided is the most beautiful environment for me. It exceeds yours and my ability to comprehend what is here and available to us when we become willing to take advantage of it. So just like the trout in our earlier trout stream analogy, if we need a bush or a tree or an undercut bank to hide from the fish hawks, those things, in my experience, are always there. All we have to do is get our minds off what's wrong with our society, our environment, and start looking for what's right for us. Then, when we need something all we need to do is look for it. And it will always be there. We have already been abundantly provided for. All we need to do is look around for the provision that has been made for us.

I'm sure you feel, "My God, that's a far-out statement." The answer is most of the time in the last two or three years I have found that to be true for me. And my vision is just starting to clear up. In the dead religions I used to hear a lot of talk about how God sends all kinds of pain and suffering. In my experience, that isn't true. In my experience, most of that pain and suffering came out of our own stubborn resistance. "I'm going to do this my way. I'm going to stay in the middle of this stream and fight this current." About then, a fish hawk makes a pass at me and leaves a two-inch wound down my back. "Oh boy, this is just part of the suffering of being a trout." No, it isn't. It's just one of the consequences of being a self-centered trout. That's what it is. Bullheaded.

The only thing that keeps an alcoholic an alcoholic is his unwillingness to say, "Help." One simple word. The minute he says, "Help," he's about 95 per cent well, the rest is just details. Until then, he's the sickest cat in the world. And I found as long as I felt, "I can do it myself, Mother," nothing good could happen in my life.

I was choosing my life. I was deciding what I was going to be. I was in charge. And boy, I sure did a great job of screwing up. As soon as I surrendered to the harmony of life and said, "Would somebody out there give me some clues as to what I should be?" I started getting the help I really needed. Jackie said, "It's very simple. You should be a teacher." My friend Bill Holbrook said I should be a teacher. And today I think I am a teacher. My students just happen to be spread around the country a little bit.

Well, those answers were lying there with Jackie and Bill for some time and I never asked. How can you get the answer if you don't ask the question? I didn't have the humility to be taught. How could I learn anything? As soon as I had the humility to be taught the teacher was right at my elbow waiting.

People say I'm lucky to have found the teachers I have here in Bozeman. The answer is yes, I'm lucky but not in that way. There are all kinds of people who have been around my teachers. Plenty of people have known Vince and Betsy and Jack and Wally but they've not paid much attention to what they had to say. Jackie and I were some of the first people who spent a lot of time listening to those folks because we were ready to be taught. When we were ready to be taught about life, the teachers were there.

What's having the humility to be taught? It's simply being ready to say, "Help me." It's simply being ready to see our mutual dependence on one another instead of denying that and saying, "I can do it myself. I'm in serious trouble when I'm thinking, I am an island, I am the master of my fate, I am the captain of my soul." No, I'm in charge of saving my own soul but I do it only with the help of my friends. I can't do this job on a desert island. I need this society I'm in.

I've studied hermits. Most every hermit I've ever seen that didn't turn sour was willing to admit, at least deep down, that he needed people. Some of them changed out of the hermit business when they saw their need for people. But by and large the story of most hermits is that they go sour, or go crazy, or turn into recluses and very destructive people to themselves and the people around them.

Montana is filled up with people who wanted to get a lot of distance between them and anybody else. And we have one of the highest suicide rates, divorce rates, and alcoholism rates in the United States per capita. And that's what comes to people who say I don't want anybody, I don't need anybody.

We're the howdy state. But twenty years later it's still howdy. That's surface friendliness, the appearance of friendliness. It's a way to avoid real friendliness. If I was to move looking for a friendlier place, I'd much sooner pick downtown New York City than any place in

Montana except Butte. But I've got my roots here with the people of Montana and the people of Bozeman. I only had to go through twenty thousand people in Bozeman to find five who liked me. That's not too bad. Five is enough.

I see now that society is very much like our ski hill. There are many beginning skiers at Bridger Bowl and to the better skiers it looks like they're really suffering as they hack their way down the hill, and bump into each other. They have almost all the accidents and broken legs. But the skiers must not be suffering too much because, no matter what happens, they come back the next year. Some of the skiers don't get much better because they don't see the need and don't ask for help. But all that's just great. They're all having a good time or they wouldn't go to the expense and trouble of going out on cold days.

There are also very good skiers on our hill. They ski like my son Joe, with a natural grace and smoothness that's a joy to watch. I don't recall that Joe has ever been hurt skiing.

As you ride up the lift and watch our hill you can focus on all the accidents, near accidents, and all the suffering from cold and fatigue. Or, you can focus on the fact that everyone is really having about as good a time as they can manage. And you can notice how, for the better skiers, there is no chaos. They don't have a problem with a bunch of people trying to avoid hitting each other. They go around the crowds or right through them, smooth as silk, not causing a problem or having a problem.

This is about the way I see society. The less I need the distraction of my escapes, the clearer I can see society and the less problems I have with it. And society doesn't need to change for this to happen to me. About three years ago, society and people stopped using me. Isn't it lovely how, when I stopped needing to be used and was willing to put that burden down, society and people around me co-operated instantly?

Many people want to yell and holler at me just for talking the way I do. But that's all right. That's lovely. If that's their idea of entertainment, let them go at me. I don't promise I'll stay and listen to all their arguments because I probably have a dental appointment I had forgotten. So they can have what they want. And I'll take the beautiful things life has for me. Right in the midst of this society that so many people see as chaos, I've found gifts for me so beautiful I wouldn't even have dreamed they existed on this earth, to say nothing of those gifts having my name on them.

EIGHT

The Scariest Thing in the World—
Emotional Intimacy

How do we move away from that part of society that's so completely absorbed with using their preoccupations to numb their pain? How do we leave behind us the only life we have known? That's one of the hardest things there is in this world and I've seen my own fear and the fears of others who have tried it. Living close to the reality, the truth and beauty of life sounds very attractive to people. But when they see the price that has to be paid many feel that they don't want it that badly.

An old Chinese proverb says, "I would rather live with the seven dragons I know than the one strange dragon I don't know." Before my heart attack, I had had a number of spiritual awakenings to life. But the life I was familiar with was too comfortable even with its terror, loneliness, and emptiness to make me willing to take a chance on the unknown.

My heart attack changed all that. It suddenly made the unknown less frightening than the known. And I think that's what hitting bottom means: when the unknown looks better than the known. We have a fear of what will happen to us if we stop controlling life. But all of a sudden that fear isn't nearly as big as the fear we have of what we have seen ourselves doing to ourselves through controlling life. That point of hitting bottom is different for every person. In the old days of AA they thought you had to lose everything before you hit bottom. They hurt younger alcoholics by telling them to go out and drink some more, they hadn't suffered enough yet. But now most of the people who are in AA see that you can hit bottom at sixteen and be ready to give up just as well as at sixty.

Emotional intimacy is so scary because we see ourselves so clearly. And we don't like what we see because it doesn't live up to our godlike conception of what we should be. What does it matter that I am an arrogant, self-centered, egotistical, cantankerous, love-starved sex maniac? There's absolutely no problem in that for me unless I'm supposed to be something else. And who says I'm supposed to be something else than that? We like to argue it's society that has that expectation. To an extent that's true, a major part of society does ask we all be angels stamped out by the same cookie cutter. But what about the big minority in society who likes a person just like me? Why isn't that enough? And there we see that playing God is the problem. It isn't enough for me that 50 million of 200 million Americans can like me as I am. I want them all.

Once I see that I'm all right the way I am, then emotional intimacy isn't scary at all because in my relationships I can get a clearer picture of what I truly am—and can make progress in my spiritual quest.

A nurse did a good job of expressing how many of us feel as we try to leave the old way behind and set out searching for a new way. As my old alcoholic friend said, "I left the herd that spent the day looking for a way to get drunk and joined the herd that was looking for another day's sobriety." The nurse said, "We, the unwilling, led by the unknowing, are doing the impossible for the ungrateful. We have done so much for so long, we are qualified to do anything with nothing. The work-aholic, doormat society."

That's beautiful. Someone in this world has to take on that load of suffering. And the fact so many are taking it on means that other people like myself can shrug it off. I would hope that none of you who are carrying that burden so beautifully would put it down because there is a chance that I might have to pick it up and carry some of it and I'd just as soon not.

This goes back to acceptance. The impossible remains impossible. There are all these dumb slogans, you know. The difficult job we do in a day, the impossible takes us a little bit longer. That's somebody who's a member of the work-aholic, doormat society.

Now I don't mean that there isn't a winning spirit, there is. And Vince Lombardi gave us a beautiful demonstration of it in a very fine way. But, you see, Lombardi did it in a different way. He said his priorities were his God, his family, and the Green Bay Packers. So winning was everything to Lombardi: everything, that is, after he had gone to visit his God each morning and been a part of his family in some way each day. Lombardi is most remembered for his saying, "Winning isn't everything, it's the only thing." What people miss is that winning was the only thing but that "only" thing was in third place in Lombardi's life.

A coach has his priorities upside down if he makes winning the first thing in his life with his wife second and church, what's that. I don't think that a coach with winning as his first priority can assemble as good a winning record as Lombardi could with winning his third priority. And I don't see such a coach having the influence of his players in their later lives that Lombardi did.

I don't see people who are successful at living peacefully and gently with their fellow men and women who don't have their own version of their spiritual quest as a high priority. This work-aholic society of ours is guaranteed to turn you into the person in Jackie's favorite quote: "She's the kind of person who gave her life for others. You could tell the others by the haunted expressions on their faces." Another line Jackie likes is, "They charge too high a price for a drink from their poisoned well." I learned not to go back to those poisoned wells. In fact, I'm getting now so I can spot some of them way out ahead of me and I can just slide sideways and avoid them. I know there's always a handy water cooler not too far away. But this again goes back to me having alternate sources. This is why we need close relationships with our five friends and family and others so we have a number of sources for our love and affection in life.

If we are fastened to one source then we guarantee our dependency on that source. Our dependency gives us a desperateness in the way we look at that source. I know that the ultimate source of our love is from our higher power and inside us. But, before I could begin to see that I had to spend years being loved by real, live people.

I had a boss who always wanted to fire me so I was go-

196

ing to show him, I was going to quit. But my friend Jerry said, "Jess, before you quit, get another horse saddled. If you have many sources of financial income, it's like having a house with many pillars. If you take away one of the pillars, then the house does not fall." So we do need a house with many pillars in our life. And oddly enough, we'll have a more loving relationship with any one person, if we have more than one loving relationship. If we have only one of what we call loving relationships, I can almost guarantee that it won't be a truly loving relationship.

It's like my only friend from earlier days. We clung to each other out of desperation like two drowning people in a huge ocean. We did everything together. We were jealous of each other's time. When we met after some years of separation, we found we didn't really care that much for each other. All we had in our relationship was a desperate need, so desperate we couldn't see we were not right for each other and so desperate that it kept the relationship from growing and becoming even as good as it could be. A house with one pillar is a very poor house.

"In view of the negative value you put on depending on one person what is your view of marriage? I know there are much nobler motivations for marriage but is it possible to be married without having a significant amount of dependency in a relationship?"

Sure, it isn't easy, but it is possible. It's very difficult because the marriage relationship is a central relationship and it had better be pretty good. Jackie and I have spent twenty-eight years together. I hope to spend twenty-eight years more. It's a renewable marriage contract, it has always been. That's no new idea. When you don't renew your marriage contract, it's called divorce, desertion, separation, murder, or living together in name only. Those things we have always had with us.

So we have to like living with each other. If we didn't we would quit. Oddly enough, it improves my marriage relationship when I see that my five friends have a certain degree of affection for me just the way I am. But I feel this will be a better day because I spent it with my wife.

Often people ask, "Jess, why can't you have only one friend?"

And the answer is, no reason except you run the risk of a dependency, but why be so exclusive? To me, the person who is capable really and truly of having one friend is capable of having three or four. The person who just wants to have one friend and wants to stand on that scares me a little bit for them. Even more scary to me is the person who wants to have one friend who is a thousand miles away. "Yes," they answer, "but we're on such a beautiful wave length."

I've got to go to the well for water two or three times a day and it won't work for me very well when there's just one friend back in Minneapolis. I've got some friends back there but I don't include them in the count of my five friends because I can't be with them one, two, or three times a week as I am with my five friends.

A lot of times when I'm talking about this stuff, it's difficult because we're talking about the deepest hunger there is here. And I know how hard it is for you. It's hard for me, too. It's no accident that I'm occasionally on the edge of tears. We're talking about deep wounds that have been there a long, long time and haven't healed. And I have compassion when some member of my audience wants to get on me and say "Shape up or ship out, you derelict. Why are you coming here and saying these things?"

They seem to want to take shots at me and show how

stupid I am and how depraved I am and they've got such a strong case. It's kind of like shooting sitting ducks.

When one of my nurses in the audience spoke openly of how hard it was for her to find the names of any friends to put on her list of friends, my heart went out to her. She was supporting me. She was saying, "Hey, friend, you're one with me, you know?" instead of backpedaling and getting herself some distance from me. I really appreciate that kind of support.

A lot of folks wonder again how I can do some of the things I do and part of the reason is that I take advantage of as many opportunities as I can, while I have them. There's a line from *Jesus Christ, Superstar* that says, "Move while you still have me." And the answer is, you and I might not be together tomorrow so if I've got some business with you, I'd better move while I still have you.

There's an old adage among us hunters, "What did you get when you went hunting?" "Well, I saw a lot of tracks." So all you eat is "track soup." And I've eaten a lot of track soup in my day. But I'm not kidding myself any more. As I said, "I'm a desperate man and this day isn't going to come around again." I've had the advantage of nearly dying three times. As I mentioned earlier, it's like Berger says in *Little Big Man,* "Once you should have died and didn't you ain't ever the same."

"Half measures avail us nothing. We stood at the turning point. We asked his protection and care with complete abandon." Those are some lines from the big book at AA. Those of you who just want to do a patch-up job, to just neaten things up a little bit, are taking a terrible risk. We are at a turning point. And half measures avail us nothing. We asked his protection and his care *with complete abandon,* which means we throw ourselves into this day with everything we have in us. We don't hold anything back.

It's just like in the old days when I was speeding all the time. I used to try to watch in the rearview mirror all the time. But I must not have been watching all the time because every once in a while, I'd look and there would be a policeman riding my tail with his light flashing.

When we've got our head buried in our navel we cannot believe, especially until much later, how much of the time that head has been buried in that navel. And sure we think we come out quite a bit. But in my experience, we don't come out in the open very much.

A serious problem we have when we try to live this new way is honesty about self. It's a crucial tool, a compass, and we've pretty well lost it. We left the virtue of honesty about self so long ago and have given it so little respect that about all the honesty we can stand on any more is that we don't steal money out of the collection plate at church. That's the only kind of honesty we've got left in us. That plus the fact we're able to be a little bit honest about the flaws in our friend's character. Those two pieces of our honesty are the last two left. It's like the endangered species. Imagine there are two water buffalo left in Africa, one in the northern tip, a male, and one in the southern tip, a female. Now that really is an endangered species. Okay, our honesty in most of our cases, was as endangered as that because it had been crowded right down to the very end.

Now, are we going to be able to reclaim that water buffalo population instantly? No. We're going to take the male water buffalo from northern Africa to southern Africa. We're very carefully going to pet it and feed and water it all the way. We're going to unite those two and sit there watching them and stroking them and feeding them and put the fan on them to cool off and see if we can tease up a little population.

The same way with honesty. That's probably one of the things I'm working hardest on today—and each day in my life. I'm trying to get a little more honesty about myself in each day.

So far I've had such magnificent fruits from my efforts that if someone asked me, "Jess, would you stand on what honesty you have now?" I'd say, "Yes, I'd be glad to. I've made enough progress, I feel so differently about my life compared to that heart attack experience fifteen years ago, I'd be glad to stand on what I have now, and keep on working with it."

But the funny thing is I know that feeling grateful about what little honesty I have is one of the things most guaranteed to bring me more. Where, if I was greedy and saying, "Higher power, why don't you give me more of this and more of that?" that's the way that produces least for me because that's the least accepting response.

So "Half measures avail us nothing. We asked his protection and his care with complete abandon . . ." This stuff I'm talking about is a program for desperate people like myself who know that their very life itself depends on the complete abandon with which we give ourselves to this simple program.

Ten years ago I was sitting in a self-disciplining group just before moving to Montana. I had been in the group for about a year. It was just like coming into a warm room on a cold day, those people were so loving and accepting to me. They liked me just the way I was. They had no program for my improvement. What held us together was the complete absence of the virtues. We were all, in one way or another, derelicts. And in that accepting group I came to see that this was where I really belonged. It was the first place I ever felt I really belonged. I didn't feel like the odd one, the one white buffalo in a herd of a million brown ones, totally self-conscious.

In one of the later meetings of that group, as I was preparing to leave, we were talking about me moving to Montana. One of the members of the group said, "Jess, remember wherever you go, there you are." In other words the geographical cure doesn't work, you take your biggest problem—yourself—with you. A geographical cure works only to temporarily distract you from your problems and the excitement of the moving, but that wears off, fast.

So in one of the last meetings I said, "What troubles me is that I don't have close emotional relationships." And this is one of the beautiful demonstrations to me of the power of an accepting group. That group didn't need to tell me anything. Because no sooner were the words out of my mouth than I realized, "Jess, you're a big fat liar. It doesn't trouble you at all that you don't have close emotional relationships. Your whole life is carefully contrived so you won't have. You have a hundred friends, ask anybody and they would say about you, 'Jess has a hundred friends.'" Yes, he does.

I'd have a friend and I would take him off the shelf and I'd say, "Let's go fishing." And we'd go fishing together. Then I'd put him back on the shelf. I'd tell him, "I'll come back in six months or a year and we'll go fishing again." And "Let's go hunting with old Bill." So he comes off the shelf and then I put him back on the shelf. "See you next fall, Bill. Really love you, really love you, man."

What I did is I had a hundred friends to avoid having any. I shuffled my so-called friends around like you had a hundred suits of clothes and you were wearing every one on rotation so you wouldn't get attached to any one.

What I had was a hundred acquaintances. And I tell you, the people who read that third book of mine, *"I Ain't Well—But I Sure Am Better,"* many of them all of a sudden got awful fussy about the use of that word friend.

So when I came to Montana after that little discussion in the group, I said to myself, "Jess, let's see if you can open up." This was five years after that heart attack. "Let's see if you can open up a little and have some closer emotional relationships."

So I met a guy just as I came to the town of Bozeman. He took me into the mountains horseback riding. And we spent some time together. Another guy was a columnist on the paper. He had a rifle like mine and wrote an article about his rifle and his shooting. I took a chance and called him up to see if he was interested in me. He was and we went out shooting together and had a good time together.

Those were my first two friends. Then I had a horrible insight. I saw it was hard for me to have a friend I didn't feel I could look down on. I had to feel superior to that person. I had to see them as inferior to me. That's some insight about yourself, just beautiful. And if you follow this program that I'm talking about, you're going to get a lot of unlovely insights into yourself. That's what makes most people quit. They slam the book shut and say, "I'm not going to take any more of this. I'm a lovely person." I want to shut the book, too. In my experience life will deal with each of us with increasing severity until we surrender and that's a beautiful alternative. But all I have to do is accept the price tag of that alternative of closing the book. As I mentioned earlier, the price tag of denying what I am is cancer or heart attacks or ulcers, but an even worse price tag is that terrible loneliness I experience when I shut the book because I don't want to look.

So I looked at myself and what these two guys were in my life. One was a bachelor and the other guy was married but only nominally. His marriage, at that time, seemed like it came about eighteenth on his list of priorities. So any time I wanted to go hunting and fishing with my two buddies, one or the other was always ready to go.

I asked my wife about this. She said, "It's simple. It takes a bachelor to keep up with you. You aren't a married man, you're more like a monk or a married bachelor. And you're more bachelor than married." It's disgusting to hear things like that from the woman who has cared for you so tenderly all these years.

And then, when one of these two guys, the bachelor, got married, my wife said, "You aren't going to see him so much any more, his wife isn't going to let him run out and play with you any time you want." And sure enough, my wife was right.

So about six months after we came here, we moved next to a guy named Dave Sullivan. And slowly, slowly, like an iceberg melting in below-zero weather, I opened up to my friend next door, Dave. Four or five years after we moved in we started to have a little better relationship. As you can see, I move very fast in these things.

After I had been in Bozeman two years, I met Jerry Sullivan and three or four years after that we started to have a real friendship. I met another man who has taught me much of what I know. I met him the first year in Bozeman, but it was four or five years before we became close.

So that's the genealogy of my first five friends. And what I found about them was they weren't people I could look down on. There is no way I could feel superior to Jerry Sullivan. He has an IQ twice my weight, he has a great skill at working with people, and he's one of the most entertaining individuals that anyone would ever have the opportunity to meet.

I did another thing. As I gradually saw how important these people were to me, I spent more time with them. One of the most horrible facts you will find as you think about this is that there have been people right at your elbow wanting to love you and you have put them off.

A friend from my advertising days came out and went hunting with me last fall. My third book—the one that spoke so much of my five friends—had just come out. Bernie and I were talking about it and he met two or three of these friends.

He said, "My God, Jess. So and so back in my little town has wanted to be my friend in the six years since we moved there. He is constantly asking me over and yet I've never done anything about it. But I really like him. And just because he isn't one of the most prominent prosperous citizens I've ignored him and put him aside."

That night he called his wife back in Minnesota and told her he was going to call the guy and get together as soon as he got back. His wife said, "Wonderful. He's wanted to be your friend so much." Until then, he had avoided the man just because he didn't think he cut quite the figure he wanted his friends to cut. Bernie's the same kind of person I am, very heavy on the showiness, very conscious of the Cadillac and the Lincoln and the big house on Lake of the Isles. That was his scene, too, when we were together in Minneapolis. When we're together, we can practically read each other's minds. We know just exactly what we are thinking. We always go for the show, we're always over on that showy side.

In my teaching when I started out I had been king on the St. Paul campus. All my students loved me. There were a few I had gotten crosswise with but mostly I was blind to my feelings and confused enough about what I believed that I was no problem to them. And some of them were ringing my chimes regularly and I didn't even know it. They were faking me right out of my tennis shoes. They were saying, "I've come to your class and found God and Jess Lair to be one and the same. And now I'm a beautiful person and thank God I came here." I'd give them their A. The quarter we were in class together I'd meet them on the way to classes and get a big smile and "Hi, Jess." Three months later it was "Hello, there." Beautiful, my it was beautiful.

It turns my stomach to look back and think about it. To think that I was that desperate and that hungry. But boy, I needed that. That was the only way I could find to get out of those places I was in. I had to face square into the wind and take what I needed and take what I could get and make the best out of it. At the end you often look back and say, "My God, was that the best I could do?" The answer for me was, "Yes, obviously it was." I was trying as hard as I could and that's the best I could do. That was the era where *"I Ain't Much, Baby—But I'm All I Got"* came from and I had to say things like that. I'd look at some of those puny, little things I was doing and some of those twisted, distorted relationships and I'd say, "Is this the best you can do, Jess?" And the answer was, "You're right, I'm trying as hard as I can and that's the best I can do." And I'd say to myself, "It ain't much baby, but it's all I got."

Like I said, I never left the virtue of honesty because I never had it that much. But even worse, the virtue I sure didn't leave was the virtue of emotional intimacy. A lot of people want to argue that kids have a lot of this emotional intimacy and emotional honesty. No way do I believe that. How often have you seen kids be deeply honest about themselves? How often have you seen kids own up and say, "I'm sure a selfish liar and a cheat in the way I took away something from my friend that was really his"? Sure kids can be honest about the other person. But that doesn't count. That's not what we're talking about here. To me emotional intimacy isn't work for children. It's men's and women's work and it is no more natural than being a ballet dancer.

There has never been a ballet star who was born knowing all the movements. The earliest you can be a finished ballet star I would guess would be in the mid-twenties. No matter how gifted physically you are there is no way that you could be a ballet star until you've spent tens of thousands of hours at the barre learning.

Emotional intimacy is not natural and it isn't work for children. I grant I'm a slower learner than most, but I don't see very many who get a good handle on their feelings in their twenties. Mostly it's the thirties, forties, and fifties before I see people doing a good job handling their feelings.

I'm a lot slower than most so I was over forty before I even started to find out what feelings were. I'll never forget my horror at a discussion we had one noon when I first came into the College of Education. We had a consultant visiting us from St. Louis. He was combining a little skiing with his consulting. A group of us education professors went to lunch with him. The topic turned to feelings and one professor expressed a question about what a feeling was. The consultant said, "What is your feeling about the fact I'm sitting in this meeting with my ski sweater on while all the rest of you are in suits and ties?"

My fellow professors puzzled over that a bit and one said, "Well, I wonder why you're wearing your sweater?"

The consultant said, "That's not a feeling, that's a thought."

At this I realized to my horror that I couldn't have come up with a feeling because I didn't know what a feeling was that well and I sure didn't know what my own feelings were at that moment.

Nine years later I can look back at that incident and I can see about twenty feelings I had but wasn't in touch with enough to get them out. I was scared, jealous, envious, mad, upset, insecure, just to name a few. My point is, see how slow a job it has been for this Norwegian to find just a few of his feelings? How can a big and important job like this be done in a few years? I'll spend the rest of my life developing more emotional honesty and emotional intimacy.

Some readers think I'm too hard on the Norwegian part of my ancestry. I don't think so. Let me tell you about a Norwegian funeral I went to some time ago. My cousin Knute had just lost his mother. He and his wife Barb were at the grave and the coffin had just been lowered. Knute's neighbors were mostly older and his mother had been a dear friend to many. And this was his mother who was dead so quickly and unexpectedly. As each couple stepped up to offer Knute and Barb their condolences they shook hands and said one word, "Sympathy." Almost every person did and said the same thing.

Their faces and the stiffness of their bodies showed their deep grief. And I know they were saying the best they could. But I don't believe we were meant to be that inhibited and withdrawn. There's silence enough in the grave. I think we were meant to be creative, outgoing personalities. I don't condemn those people. And in their lives together, I'm sure they show far more caring than will ever be possible for me. The incident and the Norwegian part of myself just serves as a little reminder of what I hope will probably be more and more left behind as I get more in tune with life.

It's like this basketball player that came out of the south, the coach's son, Pete Maravich. They said he had such a good deal because he played for his dad who was the coach. What a bunch of baloney. He spent six to eight hours a day on the basketball floor practicing, all the year round. That's some favoritism that is. Okay, what makes you spend six to eight hours a day on the basketball court, year round. All the other kids are out playing golf, or hunting, or fishing, but you're going all by yourself, to the basketball court. That's a man who's desperate for learning.

The combination here of the rewards for doing the kinds of things I'm talking about, plus the penalties for not doing them, are so great that it's enough to make anyone who looks at these things equally desperate to learn. Who can look at the rewards and not say, "Boy, that's what I want and need. I don't want to die prematurely of an imaginary illness. And I don't want to be dead on my feet any more." That's what we're talking about here, because those two are hooked together.

When you're dead on your feet, you're going to go out quick unless you have the misfortune to have an exceptionally hardy body like some of those old prunes and pickles who manage to live to ninety despite their storms of emotions. They manage to put in ninety miserable years. I can't see that they've ever brought a smile to anyone's face. They've been nothing but a source of pain and misery to the so-called loved ones around them. They have been a constant source of fighting, bitterness, jealousy, and contention, crying, whining, self-pitying, resentful old people. And then they say, "I wonder how come no one ever comes to see me?"

I saw an old lady who had a big part in killing her husband and her son with the misery and pain of her association. She turned her daughter-in-law against her and she even managed to drive her two grandsons away from her. Then she wonders how come nobody comes to see her. It's simple. She charges too high a price for a drink from her poisoned well. And why should people frustrate her lifelong desire for misery and resentment? She has fashioned those two tools as carefully as a person can fashion them. I can see now that my job is not to interfere with the laws and harmony of this life. My job is to respect them.

My students used to send me dittoed copies of an anonymous poem to the effect of love me even though I'm a porcupine, love me even though I push you away, love me even if I make it impossible for you. Love me even if I'm shy and lonely. The answer to that sick game is, no way will I do that.

I'm not in the business of loving porcupines. If you want to be a porcupine and if you want to push away the person who is carrying food to you, you have that precious right. If you're counting on me to break down your fortress, you're counting on the wrong person. The answer to you is that no one carrying any real gifts will ever penetrate your walls. The only ones who will will be the busybodies with the empty buckets. So you're going to die inside that shell of pride and self-centeredness. I must not batter down a shell. The only person who should ever take down a shell is the person himself.

I do have an obligation to reach out my hand in love and friendliness and try to awaken some poor soul but that means just that. I will reach out my hand to you within my feeble powers to do so. But, my friend, you have got to respond and meet me part way. I do not belong inside you. I used to spend a lot of time messing around inside other people's personalities with my grubby little finger straightening their personality. I'm not going to do that any more because the pain was too great and the results too fruitless.

I was not given life to save the world because that is the God business and I'm trying to get out of the God business as much as I can manage. I'm in this to save my own life and save my own soul, to make my own spiritual quest. When I start messing around in your personality that assumes I've got my own little house all cleaned up and I should be in your house.

It used to be that I would touch all kinds of people inappropriately because I was ruled far more by my need to touch than I was by the appropriateness of the touching. As that need and other needs in me got better satisfied and consequently under much better conscious control, I became more discriminating. I would only touch in a way that would be difficult or uncomfortable for the person once a month or three times a year. And now I don't see that much more than once a year do I have any indication that my touching them in some way wasn't appropriate. So you get better at something. You work at something six or seven years and you get better at it.

But you say, well, I want results immediately. But this is what life is for: learning these things. I'm in no hurry now. When I finish learning my life will be over. There is a book, *Lame Deer, Seeker of Visions*. It's about a Sioux medicine chief on the Pine Bend Reservation in the Dakotas. He had a vision as a youth that he should be a medicine man and that he would train twelve medicine men in his lifetime. He was an old man when he was being interviewed. He said, "I've trained eleven of them, and I'm in no hurry to get that last one." Isn't that beautiful? This is what our life is for, learning to live. And what a lovely way to spend it. Who wants to get nice lessons like I have each day over with quick.

I've told you about my five friends. Another crucial part of my process is my self-disciplining group. There are two kinds of groups in the world. There are groups where the members are disciplining others and there are groups where they discipline themselves only. I have found it is absolutely crucial to find a group where the members discipline themselves only and not me.

Now there are many of these groups. From what I can observe, the twelve-step ones are the ones I favor because they have a spiritual center. Most anybody can qualify for one of them because most everybody has an alcohol problem with themselves or some member of their family, a drug problem, a weight problem, or an emotional problem. There are others, Parents Anonymous is for child abusers and Gamblers Anonymous is for gamblers. To me those groups are far ahead of anything I've seen. They're hard but good.

Mowrer wrote a book, *New Group Therapy*. And the twelve-step groups meet the needs that Mowrer feels are crucial. He has been influenced by his study of AA, too. He was a very fine clinical psychologist. He was a man who had as a very young boy a sexual deviation. This was a terrible, terrible trauma to him all his life. I think it could have been the reason he became a psychologist.

Mowrer's childhood problem dogged him through the years. Finally at the age of forty-five or fifty, as he was on the verge of becoming president of the American Psychological Association, he came across something in his studies which had a great influence on him. It might have been the fifth step of the twelve-steps, which asks that you admit to God, to yourself, and to another human being the exact nature of your wrong. And he saw that maybe if he admitted what he had done it might be better. So he admitted his deviation to a group of psychologists. Now this is the typical thing a beginner at this business does, and Mowrer paid the price. He admitted his childhood sexual deviation openly. I don't know what it was, but it was supposedly gross to his fellow psychologists.

He had a terrible problem and was nearly ostracized. This is a good example of the reason you need to go very carefully at first when you try to pull the cork on some of the memories and deeds that are buried. We have a need to punish ourselves for what we see is our guilt. So we will often subconsciously set up some wrong way to bring things out and send us back into hiding again. So that's another reason why the twelve-step groups are so important. They steer you to a person they know can be trusted for the first time you say all the stuff out of the past. The person you go to is never horrified or critical. After a twelve-step group member has done this many times they have intimate friends they can trust so later there is no problem. But at first there is.

The point of saying the deepest darkest things about ourselves to another human being is we see, as we are telling the things we are so afraid of, that they aren't really very much of a problem at all. I've had people tell me that, at first, they were sure only a priest could stand to hear what they had to tell. What they had done was so awful anyone else would turn to stone. Once people see what they've done isn't so awful and they find they can get it out, they keep telling about these things until their memories lose their sting.

If I had complete emotional openness, I could write out a list of everything I had done and nail it up on the courthouse door for anyone to see. I could do that if I had a complete sense of "Ain't I a wonder and ain't you a wonder, too." But I don't have that. I haven't got enough grasp of it. Even worse, I don't have enough of an ability to practice that to be able to do it that completely.

There are other good groups in churches and other places but they are more risky. All the twelve-step groups just discipline themselves, at least they are supposed to. Occasionally somebody deviates, but it's so seldom it's not a problem usually. In the other groups, it's much, much harder to find that acceptance for you as you are. And, for most of us, when we come in at first we aren't a very pretty sight.

In other groups I see much willingness to tell people what's wrong with them and not as much willingness to talk as honestly as they can about their own feelings.

I've had my problems with some of the folks who come out of sensitivity and encounter training who say to me, in effect, "Jess, why can't you ever do the kind of things that would make you a sensitive person like me?" And I want to say, "Hey man, you're standing on my foot. Can't you see the pain in my face?"

I judge a group's values and usefulness to me by the demonstration the members of that group give me. I'm so impressed by the twelve-step groups because so many people come out of those groups who are peaceful and calm and quiet and lovely individuals and you hardly ever know they are around. They go through the water so smoothly without making ripples. So I like the way they can demonstrate what they believe in. There's another advantage to the twelve-step groups and that is that they are reasonably permanent. You know that the group will be there as long as you live.

As you can see from the stories I've told you about myself, I've got a long way to go. That's probably why I didn't die each of those three chances I had. I got sent back to do some more work.

There are self-disciplining groups in life waiting for you and there is some real value to them for anyone who is really willing to participate. Granted, there is pain and risk in opening yourself to life in a group. But the rewards are great, too, because the main reward is life itself. And the risks of not opening to life get even worse and more painful as time goes on because there is no standing still in life. We either get closer to life and people or we get further away. I'd rather try to get closer.

NINE

Making Love — the Mirror to the Subconscious Self

I spent the first forty years of my life without touching or being touched by anyone except my wife and my children under limited circumstances. Here was one of the most vital parts of human communication and I didn't even know it existed. So, in my typical bullheaded fashion I set out to learn about touching and made lots of mistakes. But what I gained and what I learned was worth for more than what my mistakes cost me. I stuck my neck out, like the turtle does, and that's the only way we can grow—to take risks.

When I found I knew nothing about touching, I could have taken one or two points of view. I could have said, "Hey, society's fear of touching put me in this bag and I'll never get out." This is the point I was trying to make about psychologists earlier. The determinist psychology says, "I'm determined, I'm trapped, I'm repressed." But I don't buy that. I'd just as soon climb out of the bag, and so I did. Not touching anyone served my interests in the earlier years. When it stopping serving my interests I was then free to change. And I could see the lack of touching was really bothering me. So I proceeded in our family and where it was appropriate to touch people. I notice now every once in a while sitting around home, I'll be sitting by one of my boys and I'll be holding his hand while we're talking.

"Touching is hard. Even touching my husband is hard. How can I make it easier?"

This question is a much bigger one than it sounds. It would have been easy to say to the lady, "Just touch your husband more." But that's a surface cure. If it would have been that simple, she would have done it herself long ago. What I have found is that we have to go deep to really find the answer to this question.

I was telling Jackie it's like a cartoon of Bil Keane, the guy who draws *Family Circus*. Little Jeffy is standing in his room and he's knee-deep in junk and he's saying to his mother, "Mother, do I have to clean my whole room or can I just neaten it up a little?"

The answer there to you folks is what I've found. When I saw the mess of my life I said, "Hey, just neatening it up a little might help some." But half measures avail us nothing. Just neatening up things a little bit is beautiful if you want to do it. But the feeling that I have is, it is very dangerous for me to be complacent or even figure I'm all straightened out now. In recent years, I've done a lot of things in my life and I've seen a lot of positive results but I can't tell you for sure what things produced the positive results. So I'm still working on the problem.

In that light, the answer to this touching problem is: I

want to show people close to me that I love them. How I can learn to do that is very, very complicated and I don't know which one of these many things I've talked about and will talk about that will make the difference. My only suggestion to you is to do them all.

Occasionally someone will say to me, "I want what you have. I can't believe some of the things you're doing. I want to be able to do things like that, would you please tell me how?" I say, "Well, I have a grave emotional problem so I do all I can with as deep friendships as I can manage and go often to my group, which is for people like me who have grave emotional problems." The guy looks at me funny and says, "Gee, Jess, I'm not that bad." He doesn't want to admit what problems he may have. But life will continue to deal with him increasingly severely. Because the most precious thing that he has is his freedom to do whatever he sees best and appropriate at the moment.

But for me, I know I spent thirty-five years not doing what was best for me. And people left me alone. My wife didn't put strychnine in my soup and the people around me didn't give me all kinds of hostility and yelling at me for not doing right. The consequences of not doing what was best for me were what paid off when I had that heart attack and I could then finally see I was on all the wrong paths for me.

So I have to let people be and concentrate on the only job my higher power has given me, which is to straighten up the mess that's inside me.

"Skin hunger, touching. We are all hungry," said one of the nurses.

When you get held lovingly, it's just like somebody's smoothing out your backbone. Somebody talks about spinal columns shriveling up and dying. That's a beautiful

218

description of someone who has "skin hunger." That's why sex is such a terrible preoccupation in this country.

In this country we are so sexually deprived ranging from our asinine birthing process up through life. The Frenchman Leboyer presents a lovely way of birthing a baby. In his method the baby is brought into life in a darkened room. It is quiet and soothing as can be. The baby is put in a warm saline solution so the feeling is much like in the womb. To me what he says is so logical and well supported that I wish we would use his ideas. But I think part of the reason we don't is that the people we have let have charge of delivering our babies are deathly afraid of things sexual. So they try to take all the feeling out and that's why hospital delivery rooms will pretty much stay the way they are.

There is a beautiful book on childbirth by the ladies down on The Farm, a commune in Summerton, Tennessee. The book is "Spiritual Midwifery" by Ina May and the other midwives. On The Farm, birthing is treated as the holy thing I feel it is and only loving people who have their heads on right are around when the baby is born. So the spiritual atmosphere is given even more attention than the physical atmosphere. We know plants can feel bad vibes from people so it's no surprise mothers and babies can. The midwives on The Farm have a fine record on birthing, better than lots of hospitals from the hard, cold facts of their success with a couple hundred deliveries. But I think there are other good things harder to measure right away.

When I was asked what was the most important thing that I've done I said it was getting rid of the terrible loneliness and stopping living a self-centered life. We need to get out of the god business and get some kind of higher power in our lives—a god as we understand him instead of as someone else understands him. I heard someone say the two basic wants that a person has are: How do you cope with the terrible loneliness and how do you cope with the desperate need to be loved? The answer, I see, is those are both the same thing. That's not two wants, it's one. Until we get out of self and let some love come into our lives, our backbones are going to shrivel up and die.

How do we get strokes? There are a lot of people using that TA word strokes in a good way. But there are some who are using it to deceive themselves. They say, "Jess, I'm giving you strokes." I want to say, "Hey, man, you may think you are, but I don't feel anything." And that kind doesn't do me any good.

The skin happens to be the largest organ in the human body. And that organ has a fantastic need for what is known as tactile stimulation, commonly known as touching. Or stroking. And boy, that takes the wrinkles out of your spine, I'll tell you. When I was in the hospital, even if I wasn't very sick, I would make sure I got those back rubs. If I could get two that was so much better than one. As near as I can figure out when I finally let the people around me get close to me, it made a big difference in my life. I let some people in, my family and my friends, and then I let all the other people in, those who have touched my life in their own way.

"My first child was a girl and I wanted to do everything right. I fed her right on schedule but I didn't touch her very much, not more than I had to. I would just go to her crib and look at her a lot. Now she's a very rigid person. With our next child, I touched her more because I was probably more relaxed and she's a real lover, a real personality. Now with the older one, I notice I'm touching her more and it seems to help, I think, but isn't it too late?"

I asked that lady to come up to the front of the room. She came up a little bit fearfully wondering what was going to happen. I put my arms around her and held her. She just collapsed and started to sob. She cried for a couple of minutes as I held her. But then she saw my wife, who was sitting in the front row, and got embarrassed. She said to her, "Is it all right if he holds me?"

I told her, "I hug nuns, I do all kinds of hugging." I told her and the group, "That's only about the deepest need we have. And that's the direct way of communicating closeness. We don't need to go through the head with speech and translate symbols down into the inside. The way to bypass the head is to go direct. It's very simple, Why don't we do more of it? That's very simple, too. We happen to be scared to death of emotional closeness, emotional intimacy. If we're going to touch somebody, we're the ones who are threatened, we're the ones who are scared, because we're going to have to get close to them.

The guys and gals on campus have found they can get someone to jump in bed with them much easier than they can get someone to open their heart to them. It's much simpler to have intercourse with someone than it is to have emotional intimacy with them. And touching, the kind of touching we're talking about, leads to emotional intimacy. It sets up an invitation and a pull towards emotional intimacy. "Don't touch me." That's the wall we've got around ourselves. That's one of the reasons our children are growing up with some of the difficulties they have.

A lady wrote an article about kids and what the young people are trying to tell us. And what she thought the young people are trying to tell us is, "Hey, I want to have it my way." They're revolting, she says. "Here's a young generation that was given more than any generation was ever given before." And you know what she shows about herself with that statement? She shows herself as a tremendous materialist, the same kind of materialist that when a kid kills the old man, the first thing you'll hear from the mother is, "We gave him everything." What does she mean? She means cars, boats, planes, football equipment, but not touching. She doesn't have that on her list. What she means is they gave him everything materially, but that isn't what kids need or want. Well, they want those material things, but that isn't what they need.

I think that lady who wrote that article is looking through the wrong end of the telescope. The younger generation that she's condemning so are selfish and self-centered just like the older generation that in her case is doing the condemning. And it's just like the generation before her, her parents. But I've got a suspicion. If I were to guess anything, I would guess our present younger generation, the people who are now in their twenties and thirties, are probably as underprivileged a generation as we've ever seen, rather than overprivileged. Sure, they have had more things than any generation that ever lived in any country that ever was. But that doesn't mean anything. It's often worse than nothing. Because when you haven't got anything to give a kid it seems like you might be a little more likely to recognize the other needs. And at least you can pretend you've done something the kid should be grateful for.

Speaking of not having anything to give, I'll never forget the story that Arnie Foss told me about his dad. His dad was a dirt-poor, scraping-the-bottom-of-the-barrel farmer from northern Wisconsin where they lived on nothing but air at times. Some of the wisdom Arnie's father had received from his dad, he was trying to pass on to his son. He said, "Arnie, if you get so that you don't have any oats for your horses at all, and practically no hay to feed them, what you should do is curry them and rub them down a couple extra times a day because that currying and touching their skin will help make up for some oats they didn't get." And that is true. I've seen people who were fighting me and yelling at me and yet I would like to say, "Hey, baby, it's going to be all right. Come and sit on my lap and I will rock you."

A lady named Elizabeth offered a course in a night university out in Seattle called Rocking. What that course consisted of was you went to her classroom at the university by appointment and you rocked in her lap. She held you in her lap and rocked you for as long as you wanted. Most people just came in the room, took a look at her in that rocking chair and ran. But some people would sit in her lap and they would be rocked and cry and then rocked and rocked.

I used to think that touching was something optional like optional equipment on a car. You had communication and then you might supplement that with touching, but it was optional.

I now see that touching is the basic communication and the talking type of communication is, in a sense, secondary.

Sex is just a special case of touching. It's just intense touching. So sex is a form of communication, about the deepest and most intense form of communication we have available to us.

One of the biggest problems in our communication is that we lack awareness of what is going on. Buried way deep in all of us is total awareness of what is going on in us and our lives. But we are often so dead to that awareness that we can't even hear the easiest part of communication, the words people use, to say nothing of all the delicate non-verbal communication.

I hear all kinds of talk about the great marriages people have. But when married couples were asked if they wished they could try over, about half wished they could. Many people want sex education taught in high school. Who is going to be able to teach the classes? The minute somebody says the word "sex," you can hear their voices go to vibrato. And the kids all say to themselves, "Wow, something big is going to happen now. Teacher's voice is shaking. And she's shaking. But she's pretending she isn't. This must really be something." The emotion of the sex education teacher, and her students, is so big and hard to handle. Here again is where communication is so touchy. That's why I've got to tell you my feelings as truly as I can. Because they are there and no way can I hide them or let them go by you unnoticed.

In my experience, while I often do a lousy job of talking about my feelings, nevertheless, it's better to do a lousy job of talking about my feelings than to deny the feelings and say I don't have any, or just ignore my feelings and hope they'll go away. I haven't found those two things to work very well for me.

L. M. Boyd in his newspaper column is an unbelievably intelligent man. I've never disagreed with him. Unbelievably intelligent. He says, "I am asked if this thing called sexual freedom is something new in Denmark? Not at all. Not at all. Even one hundred years ago (1877), the records show two out of three brides there were expecting on their wedding day." It's great that they had a chance to get acquainted.

God spare me from the iron virgin. She's the gal who walks into my office, sits her tight little fanny down and says, "That God, Jess, I have never sinned. I have held myself pure for my wedding day. Despite all the terrible pawing and pushing of the men of this day, I have resisted their overtures and I sit before you pure and undefiled. Pure as the driven snow, I sit here." And I'm just about ready to throw up. I want to say, "Look, you're a mean, hardhearted woman." She flies her technical virginity like a flag. When I was saying these things to the nurses in Ohio I had a nun with us who had taken the vow of chastity and yet didn't shove it down our throats.

To me there is all the difference in the world between the two women. One has a legalistic, narrow interpretation that is a dead, dead thing. And it stinks, to me, of false piety. The other's vow of chastity is a living thing that is very precious.

I don't wonder though that the professional virgin has her problems. When I can get calmed down a little I have compassion for her. Lots of people claim men and women were meant for each other. I can't see how they figure that.

I heard a story once that I enjoyed telling my classes about how women came to this earth. At first there were just men on earth and there was lots of hunting, fishing, drinking, and telling lies. But eventually that got tiresome so they had a meeting and decided they wanted to ask God for some excitement. So God sent down women. Right away everything quieted down with all the soft talking and love-making. But then the fighting, yelling, screaming, and pouting started. Pretty soon the men called a council and told God this was more excitement than they had bargained for. So God took the women back. The boys returned to their poker games and drinking but eventually that got dull again. So they finally met in a long and troubled council. Their decision was to tell

God to send the women back. They couldn't live with them but they couldn't live without them, either.

I'm sure women could write that story just the opposite. It seems to me there has always been a war between the sexes. About the only exceptions I've seen are for a while when people fall in love, or in very good marriages, or in the older years for some of the older married couples who didn't get along too well earlier but old age brought some peace and compassion.

I know a lot of people want to look at the world differently. That's just fine with me. I'm just telling you how the world looks to me. The reason for the war between the sexes, it seems to me, is that emotional intimacy is hard with people of the same sex, but it is the hardest between sexes because that's where it can be the deepest. I see that when we make love, most all of what we are comes into play and shows itself. And that's what we can't stand. Our love-making is the clearest mirror we have of ourselves and we hate so much to see ourselves because in the clear mirror our love-making hands us we can't continue to see ourselves as the gods or goddesses we have been believing we are.

Let's look at the words "making love." What they literally say is that it is love we are making. The question that then comes to mind is what quality is the love we're making? When we look at sex this way, I can see why the expression "having sex" is much closer to the mark than "making love." Unfortunately this applies to much of sex in marriage as well as to sex outside of marriage.

To me if you want to look at a group of people which you don't want to be like, go look at the psychological profiles of the swinging couples. Talk about a shallow, non-emotionally intimate life style both with their swinging partners as well as in their own marriages.

A lot of people tell me they like the ideas in my book. I tell them, "You should because I took them from the very best livers of life I could find." And I tell you, I'm not looking at any swinging couples for beautiful life styles that I want to copy. Because when you look at those lives carefully and you want to hold that out as an example of psychological maturity, you've got rocks in your head. To me that's the shallowest kind of emotional living. You'll see the lives they lead are terrible messes, if you look carefully.

There haven't been very many follow-up studies done on swinging, but I have run into a few. Check on swinging couples ten years later and you see one of the big problems with this sex business. There's so much lying and so little truth-telling. Everybody is putting each other down. Everybody is bragging about all their sexual exploits. And they are just a big bunch of liars.

It's like when I was in the Army. These dark, curly-haired guys would come in late at night and say, "Wow, what a great night of sex I had." I sat there, young, frightened, and envious. And later I might see one of these good-looking cats sitting in the USO reading a magazine. He didn't even have the guts to ask the hostess to play ping-pong with him. I at least had that much guts. But he would come in that night and make his big brag again. I thought to myself, "You liar. I saw you at the USO and you were just reading magazines." But I didn't say anything.

Then I noticed another funny thing. There were these brown-haired guys who came in early Monday morning. They were so tired the guys on either side had to prop them up for reveille. They would go back to sleep for the day because they had paid off the top sergeant so they didn't need to do duty Mondays. On a weekend, I'd see these guys driving around town with four girls in a convertible. And they didn't say anything about their sex life, ever. They just sat around real loose with a big smile on their faces.

So then I started to realize how much sexual conversation is worth, which is nothing, just nothing. It's such a terrible hurt because here is one of the crucial parts of our communication and no one will tell the truth. No one will tell even their own brother the truth, that sex is really a tough deal. That's why my next book will probably be on sex, if I find I know enough about it, called *"Sex, If I Didn't Laugh, I'd Cry."*

It's hard even to touch other people because of the threat of emotional intimacy. The toughest of all kinds of touching is sex because even though you can do sex without emotional intimacy, eventually, if there isn't some emotional intimacy, sex just turns to ashes.

A student of mine had gone back to this hospital where he had worked. He met a nurse, a doctor's wife, with whom he had a tremendous closeness. She gave him this big, warm, and very sensual hug. That night he was having intercourse with his girl friend and he realized to his horror that there was more closeness between him and the nurse he was hugging that afternoon than there was with the gal he was having intercourse with. That turned him off. His gal wanted to know what was wrong. He wouldn't tell her and that made it worse. Finally she squeezed the truth out of him. When she found what his feelings were she came unglued. Then they started to really open up and talk and get some emotional intimacy into their relationship.

In one of my early classes, a gal student said, "Jess, I can see what you're up to. My boy friend and I had been having sex almost from the start. But we had been using sex to cover up some of the emotional problems that were between us. So I kicked him out of bed and we're getting to work on what those emotional problems are. And he feels kind of rejected because he doesn't have this class to help get his head straight about it. But we're trying to hash out these emotional problems that are between us."

So true emotional intimacy is the hardest thing there is. And of course, unless there is true emotional intimacy, sex can't be anything more than a very physical kind of thing.

There was a television show on prostitution. When I watched the show, I was so horrified to find you're not supposed to kiss the prostitute. A prostitute took a customer to a room and another gal was there and they were arguing while she was undressing. The guy finally said, "Well, what about me?" "Well, I'll get to you." So she kept taking her clothes off. He went to embrace her and she said, "No, kissy, kissy." You can have intercourse with her but you can't kiss her. There again is a good example of how you can take what should be the most crucial part of emotional intimacy and so isolate it that it's unhooked from any kind of emotional intimacy.

A review of the book *The Female Orgasm* by Dr. Fisher says, "Dr. Fisher's positive finding is that the greater a woman's feeling that love objects are easily lost or may disappear, the less likely she is to attain orgasm." This kind of anxiety goes right into that we're talking about.

When you had the kind of friends I used to have where they were gone tomorrow morning at a moment's notice because the association was that tenuous, and there was no true intimacy, there was no true closeness in there, of course you'll have the feeling that this relationship is tenuous. You've got enough sense, at least, to know deep down what the problem is. The kind of relationships I'm talking about here are not tenuous. They give the two people involved a tremendous sense of security in the relationship.

Each of us can have any kind of relationship we want. They can be as solid and secure as we want them to be and as we will allow them to be. As our ability to tolerate emotional intimacy increases, our relationships will get better. And how do you do that? The same way you learn ballet, by practicing.

I'll never forget a gal who attended a seminar my wife and I gave in Portland, Oregon. The gal said, "Jess, I've always been afraid of guys. I had one marriage and it was such a casual thing on both parts it busted up quick. I want these things you're talking about so badly, but how can I learn to love guys?"

"Well, honey," I said, "would you believe that for someone with your kind of track record and your kind of inexperience, you very possibly might have to start with one-night stands and gradually work your way up."

This horrified her. She was a beautiful lady of quality. She should immediately be able to jump into a high-class, long-term relationship. But in feeling this way she's playing god. That's a fairy tale that shows no respect for the realities of love, absolutely no respect at all. In one way or another, everybody pays the same price for their ticket and the price of these tickets is blood and tears—and years and years of time. Anyone who tells me they got their ticket for nothing or by just snapping their fingers is a big liar. I've never seen it happen.

So I was trying to tell this lady what learning the world of reality and coming to an association with men would be like starting with one-night stands. After a year or two of that she might get so she would be able to go with a guy for two or three weeks. After that something better might happen. At first she was just horrified. But then I said, "Look what a lovely time you're going to have practicing." And she could see the hope in it. Because if she's paying attention, she's going to get something out of it. She finally saw that while she was afraid of looking at learning sex the best way she could, she was even more afraid of living with her childish illusions, so now she could get started. Now I don't mean everybody has to learn about sex in a hard and brutal way. Many people can keep their illusions and find something pretty close to what they hoped for. All I'm telling you is what seemed to be the best thing for me to say to this one woman.

One of the most striking examples of this was one of my students at Minnesota. As a freshman she was in such bad shape that she was it for a couple of gang bangs with a bunch of fraternity guys lined up outside the door to have intercourse with her. She got to the point, after a few of those, where she didn't need that any more. She progressed to one-night stands, then to running around with a guy for two or three weeks being very possessive and desperate. Her sorority sisters were trying to shape her up. She was telling me at that stage of her life, "If a guy didn't ask me to go to bed with him on the first date, I figured he was a queer." But she outdid all her fellow sorority sisters. She went through these progressions so fast that within two years she was going with a really nice guy and they were talking abut getting married. But she told me she kept picking fights with this serviceman she loved. She said, "Jess, why do I do that?" I said, "Simple. You're trying to say to him, 'I'm no good for you. I'm not worthy.' "

She said, "You're right. I did. And by gosh, I am worthy, aren't I?"

I said, "You're right. You've paid for your ticket, honey." And she understood what I meant. She married the guy and had children. I wouldn't be surprised if she hasn't got a lot better marriage than some of those sorority sisters of hers who found all their pretty illusions weren't true and they found they couldn't hold a marriage together. I've seen a number of stories very much like the one I just mentioned. Hers is just a little more spectacular in its details but the essence of the stories is the same.

I believe in God's world, which has a beautiful order and harmony. Now it isn't just the kind of purity and perfection and simplicity that we're asking for in our making ourselves God. We decided how this system should be. Oh, it should be a lovely system. And all the courtships are full of flowers and violins and candelabras. That's the way it's supposed to be. Who says so? Well, I say so. Great big self-centered I, that's who.

God doesn't run the universe that way. It's just like if my group of ninety psychiatric nurses and I all decided we would be ballet dancers. Our ages were twenty-two to seventy-two and weights were eighty-five to two hundred and eighty-five. Do you think that would be a sweet and lovely process? Look at the pain we would have to go through. Look at the weight I'm going to have to lose. I've got two left feet. I've got no hand-eye co-ordination. I've got three thousand things against me. Twenty years from now I won't have made much progress in ballet. You can imagine how little I'll know in only ten years. That's reality. And very few have tried to deny the reality of ballet because it's out in the open. But if you can't see it, it isn't there. We know how hard it would be to go from where you and I now are to the ballet dancer who can execute all the basic movements with fluidity and grace. But that's what we're talking about doing in a

232

harder art than ballet, the art of loving. Ballet isn't easy but we're ready to submit ourselves to the beautiful order of the universe which is our limitations in action.

Now why can't we be ready to do this with the other things of life like learning to love, which is the most important thing there is and far more important than learning to be a ballet dancer? Let's learn to love the way we have to learn to love instead of the way we want to learn to love. Let's look at what kind of lovers we really are instead of what kind of lovers we want to think we are. There is a beautiful way of telling what kind of lovers we really are and that's how many people want to be around us. Before, I couldn't have collected three friends without $10,000 each to buy them off. Nobody wanted to be around me on my best days. Now, once in a while, there's an occasional person who would just as soon be somewhere near me. So I'm getting to be a little bit better lover.

Have I got problems as a lover? I've got all kinds of problems. I could name you all kinds of limitations in all my loving relationships. I have been weighed and in those respects found wanting. How long will those limitations persist? I don't know. Am I working on them? Yes, I am, as hard as I can. But I am limited by what I can change and what I can do. And then the higher power has to step in and fill up as much of the gap as he chooses to fill up on his own time schedule. Will he make enough changes in me fast enough so they are made in time? The answer is he will because I have faith and patience with that higher power and his time schedule is always much better than mine. And the higher power knows what needs to be done far better than I do.

So I will take the same tough medicine that I talked to the lady about who asked me how to learn how to love.

And I will learn this business as well as I can, the way it has to be learned without living in illusions and delusions and without lying to people. And worst of all, when we lie about sex we lie to friends because they are the only ones we talk about it all to. What kind of friendship is that when the people who are dependent on us are the ones we most lie to? When we say to a friend, "I'm such big stuff, and you must be some kind of jerk because you can't measure up to my lies," we sure don't have very good relationships.

I have found that it is nearly impossible for people to tell me the truth in the sexual areas of their lives. A few people have done that for me—that deep kindness. And calmed me down by doing it. They have told me about reality instead of their own fantasies which they think are real. The only way they could think those foolish fantasies were reality would be to lie like hell to themselves.

Anaïs Nin, a great lady, who wrote *The Novel of the Future*, says, "I go out to a party and meet the editors of *Partisan Review*. They sit there with unsmiling, cold faces, uninviting, closed. Their talk is harsh, ideological, political, dry, neither warm, nor human, nor sensitive. They are tough intellectuals without the slightest charm or wit or humor or tolerance. They are rigid, clever in a cold way." And that's a typical college professor party, the big intellect at its very highest. And if there was ever something I most wanted not to be it would be that.

She goes on, "Women are so much more honest than men. A woman says, 'I am jealous.' A man covers it up with a system of philosophy, a book of literary criticism, a study of psychology."

I have never seen a woman crazy enough to be a philosopher. And talk about a dry, moldering dust, that's

234

it. Too much philosophy rots the mind. What Nin says is crucial to intimacy because the most common way to escape from feelings is to go into the head, into the intellect. It's rare to see a man who lives too much in feeling. Almost all men live too much in their heads and are too cold. Most of the rest of them live too much in their bodies and are too brutal. And since we dummies are half of that heterosexual sex, that means that all of us who are living in our heads or our bodies can't participate very well in the flowery combat of sex with all its beautiful feelings.

Nin continues, "I believe that man created art out of fear of exploring woman. I believe woman stuttered about herself out of fear of what she had to say. She covered herself with taboos and veils. Man invented a woman to suit his needs. He disposed of her by identifying her with nature and then paraded his contemptuous domination of nature. But woman is not nature only. She is the mermaid with her fishtail dipped in the unconscious. Her creation will be to make articulate this strange world which dominates man, which he denies his domination by but which asserts its domination in the destructive proofs of its presence—madness.

"If a person continues to see only giants, it's because he is looking at the world through the eyes of a child. I have a feeling man's fear of woman comes from having seen her as the mother creator of heaven."

To me there is a very legitimate fear back and forth between men and women because they are very different. And men and women are not suited to live together. But even more, they are not suited to live apart, so they make the best of the deal and live together as well as they can with the deepest attempt on both parts, hopefully, to understand and be compassionate for the differences in each other.

In one of his columns, "Reflections of a Square," John Ciardi says, "For one hundred dollars plus the requisite amnesia of what the human race has been dreaming about since the start of things, you may buy a key to the Playboy tower of fun in New York. Your key paid for, you may then buy your drinks at $1.50 apiece on the promise that you will overtip everyone, but especially the bunny who is assigned to wink her assemblages at you with the understanding that it is poor form to wink back and utter social ruin to touch or even think of touching. What you pay for, plus tips, is the basic male freedom to have nothing to do with sex when it is waved at you all over the place.

"A Playboynik is there to play it cool. No hot, little hands, no hot, little thoughts. Mr. Hefner said, 'Cool, man, cool.' And Mr. Hefner has piled up something like fifteen million dollars, utterly detached but highly communicative dollars showing you what he means."

At one point in his article Ciardi mentions that one other sin that must not be committed in Playboy Club is uncertainty. Thou shalt not commit uncertainty.

In my experience, Ciardi's story is not just common, it's the overwhelming majority's reaction to sex and handling of sex. Sex is one of the most powerful, positive, constructive possibilities there are, yet it is made mechanical and degraded because typically both of the parties do not want the other person to get close to them. Don't touch me, not so much in the sense of don't touch me physically, because you have to to have intercourse, but "don't touch my heart."

The new sexual freedom so flaunted and talked about is

a flight from intimacy. The sexually free person of ten years ago is already often trying to tell his or her psychiatrist why they feel such a terrible loneliness, or guilt, or why they are trying to punish themselves. We used to have some emotional intimacy and then sex. Now we have sex as a means to try to avoid emotional intimacy. Quick sexual intercourse is a great way to avoid emotional intimacy or cover up the lack of it.

But I don't give much meaning to all the so-called sexual trends. To me those changes and trends are just on the surface. What's underneath is what's really important. And I see the young people in our colleges the last fifteen years as being just like their parents' generation. Sure there's a lot more intercourse. But let's not stop there, let's go deeper. Both the sexually free and inhibited college students deep down are just as scared and afraid of emotional intimacy as their parents were, my generation. I've talked to guys and gals who have had intercourse hundreds of times and they didn't win any freedom for themselves. They are just as bad off as or worse than the inhibited students and there are still plenty of them. It's just that no one will believe me when I try to tell them that. How can a girl who hasn't gone out with a guy for three years have intercourse very often? If you looked at her, you'd say, "There's a pretty, young swinger." The truth is she's so afraid of boys she can hardly talk to them.

I just can't see that things are really much different today than they were in that old history book, the Bible. It's packed with the same kind of problems I see in Bozeman, Montana. To me there's only one question: are we going to come out of our self-centered self or aren't we? If we come out of our self-centered self, the only person there is to meet is our higher power—God. To me that's the eternal problem.

I can pass my money to my kids when I die. And I can pass some knowledge to them because knowledge is cumulative. We don't need to keep rediscovering fire or reinventing the wheel. But one thing, fortunately, I cannot do for my kids is I cannot make their spiritual quest for them. There are some things a man or a woman has to do for themselves. You blow your own nose, you say your own prayers, and you make your own love.

I notice that many of the people who write me about my books turn first to the chapter on sex. At least one third of all the questions I get are on that topic.

I think the problem is our fear of our feelings about ourselves and the way sexual intimacy threatens our feelings. In Studs Terkel's book *Working* he tells about the prostitute. She turned her sexual feelings off when she had sex with her customers and then turned them back on when she had sex with her boy friend. After a while she was horrified to find she couldn't turn her feelings back on.

I don't think we have to share her predicament. I think, no matter how turned off our feelings are, that we can get back in touch with them. And as Anaïs Nin says, "Men need women to help them." I believe Nin's figure of a woman being like a mermaid with her tail in the unconscious is a useful one and can often mean a chance to complete ourselves. I would suspect, too, that there is a chance men, if they would truly open themselves and their feelings to women, might be of some use to women in completing themselves. So this is how I see that men and women together are so needed in each other's spiritual quests. And this means spiritual sex. Then we see sexual union as one more thing, that while good in itself, also has a higher usefulness. But we need to become ready to put down our fear of each other and to be willing to give up trying to run the world our way—trying to be our own god.

TEN

The Mind-body-spirit Harmony:
The Inner Perfection in Each of Us

The mind-body-spirit harmony that is each of us is to me what we're seeking. We're like a three-legged stool. The only problem is two of our three legs go out from our stool in such wildly different directions that our stool won't stand. The spiritual leg is the dominant leg. Only the spiritual side of us can show us what is best for the body and mind. So we need to get the body and mind legs of our stool in harmony with the spiritual leg. Then our stool will stand. All you need to do is look around you and you'll see almost constant examples of what I'm talking about.

In our local paper recently was a picture of the nursing class of 1940 who graduated from the local Bozeman hospital. All but two or three of those twenty-two women were carrying a lot of extra weight. A group of men from the same year would probably show a lot more of the same thing. I don't mean there's a special virtue in being thin. But what I see as we get more in harmony, body, mind, and spirit, the less trips we have to make to the cookie jar.

I don't want to make too big a thing of weight because fat is just one of the many clues that show us that we are out of balance. Fat is just so easy to talk about because it is so obvious, and because in its extreme form, it's so dangerous. All the health experts pretty well agree that we die way too soon, twenty to forty years prematurely. The reason isn't just being overweight. The reason is our whole life is out of harmony and our weight is just one of the symptoms. Just watch people walking down the street. Look at how many sad or crabby faces you see. Look how stiff and tense people move. That isn't something to be solved by a calisthenics. No matter how supple your muscles are, if you're frightened or angry you won't move smoothly. So a bigger clue to our mind-body-spirit harmony than our weight is the look on our face and the way our bodies move. Those clues are just a little less obvious and harder to read.

An interesting example of this is in the town down in Ecuador where it is so common to have old people. There are a great many people over a hundred years old. They are extremely active up into the 120s and some are still sexually active at 100. It's not heredity that makes the difference; the experts say only 5 to 10 per cent of that can be due to heredity. So we know it's something other than heredity. It shows me that our bodies have the genetic capability of a very long and active life. It's so interesting to me because we see again a physical manifestation of what we have done to ourselves when we see the rapid decay of our bodies so common in this country. A person who is forty years old in America has

241

less life expectancy than a man of forty in Bolivia. That's the price we pay for our way of living. And this is despite all the medical advantages we have working in the later years that Bolivia doesn't have. Almost all of our increase in life expectancy for adults has come about by wiping out the infectious diseases, principally tuberculosis, which in the early 1900s was the biggest problem.

Why are we dying so fast? I saw an obituary the other day for a lady who died at fifty-four of natural causes. How can you die at fifty-four of natural causes? This statement was a polite way of saying she didn't blow her brains out with a gun. But she most likely committed suicide in the same way I was in the process of committing suicide. So old age shows us what our problems were earlier because eventually we can't deny them any more. When we're young and strong, we can deny. "Oh, no, I don't have a problem." The community in Ecuador shows us the genetic structure of our bodies is really perfect. We know our spirit is perfect. And there's really nothing wrong with our minds at first. So the problem is we're not in harmony.

In our early years our "I-ness" gets stronger and stronger and there gets to be a separation between the "I" and the rest of us where disease and sickness can come in. We need to get the parts together and working in harmony because I am my body, I am my mind, and I am my spirit. The more they are in harmony, the more I am. So our bodies show what we are inside. My fat, my scars, my angry face, my stiff shoulders, all of these show what I am inside. One of the things though that I find so beautiful about the human organism is that it is like a very complicated piece of machinery. If you want to stop it, you can put a stick in the gears any place and stop it. If you want to smooth out the machinery, you can start oiling it any place and the whole machine will run a little smoother. Same way with the body-mind-spirit. If you want to change it, you can approach it in a number of ways. One of the things you could do to develop your spirit is to take dancing lessons. Because the body and the spirit are hooked up together, a way you can improve your body is to learn something new for the mind. We're all part of the same thing. And we're always looking for harmony.

The best way I've found to get in harmony though is to work directly on the area that we are most out of harmony with. As I mentioned, for me this means work on the spiritual part a lot and the body some to bring them into harmony with my relatively overdeveloped but confused mind. I have found that what little work I have done to develop the spirit has helped clear my mind and expand my awareness. And it has helped heal my body.

Developing the mind is usually no problem because it is frequently overdeveloped. I thought, looking back at my days as a student at the university, that most of us were educated way beyond our intelligence.

When it comes to getting in harmony with the spirit, it's hard to find people who are too much in harmony with their spirit. There's where our groups are so crucial. I go into my self-disciplining group two or three times a week so I can count on spiritual conversations. Plus anytime during the week that I need those people, they are there. Plus, I have the five friends.

The study done on medical students that I mentioned earlier wraps this harmony idea up so well. The study was started thirty years ago on a group of medical school students who are fifty or over now. There was a certain group of people who had the withdrawn personalities and they got cancer. The aggressive personalities had heart attacks and inhibited personalities got the ulcers. One thing they found was very interesting. There was a group of people who had high cholesterol counts but they were creative, outgoing personalities and they didn't have heart attacks. Oddly enough they had the best success in their medical practices, too. And the thing they found, one of the most interesting characteristics about them, they had a strong sense of their mutual interdependence. They were not alone. They were actively in relationships with other people.

It seems to me, this is the central issue for me. Will I come out of myself into relationship with you? To me, all my compulsions serve to hide me from that very thing. Any time we take the beautiful things of life like work, sex, play, religion, and turn them into an obsessive-compulsive activity, to me that's one of the most terrible things we can do. We have taken a beautiful thing and destroyed it. We feel we need all those compulsions because they help us take our mind off looking at ourselves. And because we're trying to be God, we don't want to look at ourselves and see how far short we fall.

We need others but the problem we have is, if we get into a relationship, it forces us to see what we are. A relationship is a true mirror in which I see myself as I am. And I don't want to see myself as I am. It's too frightening and it's too hard for me. But we need to get into association, we need to get into mutually interdependent relationships so we can start saving our lives and so we can make today count.

Now you say, "How can we do this when our communities are so fragmented where everybody is running away from each other?" A tape-recorded study of American conversations on jobs, at school and at church meetings found that only two sentences out of each hundred were about the feelings of the person talking. The other ninety-eight sentences were about ideas or statements or questions. The sadness is those conversations were carried on by people just like you and me and the other members of our communities. So who can we find to talk feelings with so we can have a real community? The answer is we simply find in our communities those people who want to be in association with us and we build a little community within our community and if there are people in that community who do not want to be in association with us or with anyone else, that's fine. That's their business. I have found no area where there aren't enough people who can make life much more of a joy, every day. And, of course, it means you live longer. But that's really a side benefit. The main benefit is a lovely day today and tomorrow in close association with lovely people.

One of the big problems our marriages have is that marriage is the only relationship we have that amounts to anything. And that's one of the reasons that when a spouse dies, the other person often dies quickly thereafter. What is so tragic is that if you could tell the person who died first that their dying would be so hard on their marriage partner, the person who died first would think, "My God, I didn't know that. I would have guessed from their attitude that they would have been so happy to see me go. Why didn't they tell me I meant so much to them while I was still around?"

The sadness is, while the marriage relationship is the best one we've got, it often isn't very good. There isn't much we can say about it while we're around. It goes back to this dependency problem. When there is only one relationship it carries such a terrible burden that there is no way one relationship can live up to all we ask of it. And there is a dependency instead of love. Husband and wife drift alone in a sea of strangers. But in that context it doesn't seem to me that the husband-wife relationship can be good because they have to be so involved in each other's lives with no outside emotional support that there is bound to be jealousy, possessiveness, envy, and resentment. And when two people have to be all things to each other, it's no wonder they fail. In a big survey of marriages, over half weren't very happy with their marriage. Yet, when that marriage is threatened with death or divorce, it nearly kills the other. Weak as that relationship is, it's the best we have.

And I think we see here, too, where that marriage has to be set in some kind of community for it to be at its best. When each of the partners in marriage have the strong support of the community, the "protective wall of human community" that Carl Jung mentioned in his letter to Bill W., then each partner can get nourishment and support from that community. And in that situation, a great deal of jealousy, possessiveness, and other negative feelings aren't so likely. When an individual has ten to twenty strong emotional relationships in community with sons, daughters, relatives, and friends, then the behavior of the marriage partner isn't as threatening and frightening as when there is only one relationship.

I think that is essentially the reason for the high longevity in the isolated communities, those old communities I spoke of. I think the other health factors are a natural side effect of the community rather than that the health factors created the other good things in the community.

If all this is so, what could possibly keep us from enjoying all the lifetime benefits of community? I think it's the same thing that makes our marriages so poor and makes our personal lives so empty. In our self-centeredness we turned inward. We stayed there out of fear. We used our rational mind to try to figure a way out and all we ended up with were sick money, power, and glory games to try to get something in our life to take away loneliness.

But none of these things work and we've got a ton of evidence to prove it, but few are interested in the evidence because it contradicts what they want to feel. We all want to think that if we had more money, a better job, a better wife, a healthier body, we would be happier. They don't see that there are all kinds of people who have more money, a better job, a better wife, and a healthier body who are just as miserable as they are.

I have seen that only "hitting bottom" can change our lives. Hitting bottom is when the unknown looks better to us than the known. Finally, the unknown of living the spirit-centered life looks better than the known life of the self-centered life. Only when we see we can't, with our rational mind all by ourselves, figure things out and control things, can we begin. Only when we finally turn to that still, quiet voice in each of us and humbly submit to that voice, can we make progress. I'm speaking of the spiritual conversion that Jung spoke of, but conversion isn't the best word because it suggests converting from one kind of spirit to another. I think spiritual awakening is a better word because it suggests awakening more and more to the spirit that has been waiting there in neglect all this time.

Because we are mind-body-spirit combinations. Unless the voices of all three parts of us are listened to and respected we can't be whole people. And here is where my science, psychology, has been so wrong. It has made listening to the spiritual voice such an object of scorn that even the great Jung in the last year of a long life was still afraid to speak out openly and strongly for the spirit because of what his colleagues would say. It is not very hard for me to say these things because psychology for me has never been anything but a tool and a meal ticket. I don't worship it.

I got my Ph.D. in psychology only so I could move to Montana and teach. So the fact that, from my experience, many psychologists would scorn these ideas, doesn't keep me from saying them openly.

The other problem we have with speaking of the spirit within has been created by our ministers and congregations. So many horrible things have been said and done to people in the name of religion and of the spirit of Christ that the mention of the spirit or higher power in a twelve-step meeting is enough to drive many new people right out of the meeting and it might be years before they come back, if ever.

But the spirit I speak of knows no denomination. Mostly the spirit is addressed as just spirit without all the capital letters and fancy names. And the spirit replies. Or, the spirit is addressed as any of the religions of the West or the East and the spirit doesn't seem to mind, it still replies.

One of the advantages of living in a small town is you can watch people's lives over a long period of time. And I see a very interesting thing. If you were to ask me the names of the twenty people in Bozeman I see touching people's lives in the most loving and gentle way and not creating problems for people, there would be only one minister on the list. Many people on the list are following their spirit in such a quiet way that I don't believe even they think of it as such. But those people lead the beautiful lives of letting go and trusting that have changed their lives and the lives of the people fortunate enough to be around them.

The biggest thing I see in people leading these beautiful

lives is acceptance. Each of them has accepted that they aren't very much. They are just a plain accountant, or a teacher, or a dentist, or a guide, or a parts man, or a news dealer, or a minister and that ain't much. But that acceptance and letting go is a slow and steady movement away from their self-centeredness. I think each of them is following their spirit as I'm trying to follow mine. But always my enemy is going back into self-centeredness where just the mind and the body talk and don't let the spirit have its turn. So I see the enemy as my self-centeredness and my goal as the mind-body-spirit–centered self.

When we're self-centered, we've got to control everything so it all comes out perfect. And we're trying to be perfect. But we can't be perfect. It's impossible to be perfect. Yet it frightens us not to be controlling everything perfectly. So we continually try to narrow the world down more and more and limit the world and control the world so we can be perfect and everything will work out just the way we want it.

A lady was telling me about her husband. "I want him to be where *I* want him to be. I want him doing what *I* want him doing, when *I* want him doing it." But there is no freedom for the other person that way and none of us can ask that of the people around us.

But this is what we do when we try to be perfect. The only way we can be perfect is we've got to control everything, make it all come out just right. That doesn't work. And because it doesn't work, life threatens us, life frightens us, and life just doesn't suit us.

While we can't be perfect, we are perfect beings right now. Every one of you is an absolutely perfect being right now. You and I all have hidden within us the potential, just as we are, without changing anything to live to be 120 in a happy, healthy, mutually interdependent, productive life as creative outgoing personalities. And not only so we live to be 120, but those are 120 good years, all the rest of them between now and then.

We are all potentially perfect beings within, when we get out of the center and let our being develop just exactly as it was meant to be. Now, the consequences of this are drastic. One of my students, Robbie, was a twenty-year-old girl studying dancing. What I'm saying means that Robbie is going to be a beautiful, beautiful dancer and float like a leaf. And her sister is going to be something else lovely, developing along her own special lines. Then the third sister is going to do something else lovely, developing in her own special way.

Every one of you has already had or is going to have some of the same experiences I've been experiencing recently which is not just work that I love, but a whole life that I love, filled with lovely, lovely things for me. And sure, everything isn't going the way I wanted it to in the old self-centered way of controlling. Everybody isn't doing just what I expected them to do. But something far better than that is happening.

Instead of having very little as I did under those old terms, or nothing, because nothing would work out just the way I wanted it to, I now have a fantastic abundance. By letting go of the people around me, many of them are doing better things for me than I ever could have dreamed possible. And I now have moments where I'm experiencing that I am a perfect being. I am perfectly human. Some of the things that people around me, and especially the people I rub the wrong way, might think are my defects of character, those are simply the things that confirm my humanity. If I had no defects of character, I would be a god. And if I were a god, there would be no place for me on this earth. I would not be a perfect human being. I would be a god.

My human imperfections are what make me exist on this plane, on this human plane, during the time I will have a physical body rather than just be pure spirit, which I was at some time and which I will be again at some time in the future. I will change from the physical body and spirit and mind all tied together into just the spirit going off by itself with perhaps some traces of the body and mind carried with it. But the shell certainly will be left behind.

So I am a perfect human being just as I sit here. And I have seen enough of a totally different way of life, I have experienced enough of it to know the fantastic potential for me that I've already seen. So far the glimpses I've had have given me just a dim picture of what might lie ahead.

I don't have to have any more than I have now. I don't have to experience any more than I have now. But oddly enough, the more grateful I am, the more content I am with what I'm presently experiencing, the more I will be given.

I have been happy with this day, and I know the odds are about 999 out of 1,000 that I'll be very happy with tomorrow and the other days ahead because that's been the situation. So, we can't be perfect. There's no such thing as being perfect, but we are perfect beings, perfect human beings.

Now some of us carry many marks of our past. I happen to have a big zipperlike scar from my neck all the way down to the bottom of my belly. The first half they opened up to do the heart, and the second half they opened up to do the stomach. I've got other scars where the chest tubes went. My scars are a reflection of what I did to myself as I escaped into myself and lived in my self-centered self where I tried to control the world and then ran away from the emotional pain into work. That's how I produced my coronary.

I happen to have congenitally small coronary arteries. They found this out when they did the X-ray studies for my heart surgery. So the kind of pace I lived at coupled with those congenitally small arteries brought my heart attack on at such an early age. However, even with those congenitally small arteries, I could have lived to be 120 had I, at a very early age, seen my self-centeredness and come out of it and gone over to a higher-power–centered existence.

We had a man in the town next to us die. When they did an autopsy they found his coronary arteries had been so clogged for years that he had almost no blood available to his heart. But because he was living such a peaceful and serene life by then, there was never any strain on his heart beyond the level of his heart to handle it. There were no outbursts where he tensed up in anger and fear. And there were none of those deep depressions that so often precede and cause a heart attack. So he was able to get the maximum use out of those fragile little heart arteries.

Life really starts when we begin to get out of self. Much as I see this, I can't bring anyone out of having self at the center point to where they have a higher power at the center point. I can't do that for anybody else. Much as I love my wife and my children, I can't do this for any of them. I can't even make the judgment that they aren't already out of self. My only responsibility is to do it for me. And then they take care of whether or not and when they want to do it. Now getting out of the center point is contagious. It's like having colds and flu going in the family. You can catch one but you can also catch the other.

What could a teacher of psychiatric nursing like my nursing friend Esther do to communicate this to her nurses so they could communicate it to their patients? The answer is very simple. She could talk some about it, but 90 per cent of it is being it. And in this case, Esther was already being that. Otherwise, she couldn't have been as radiant as she was during our time together. She's out of the center or she couldn't have been in such harmony with me and other people around her as I observed her there.

So we need to follow people like Esther who have done so much of this and follow them in a humble spirit and say, "Look what Esther has done. Why don't I do more of that?"

And there was Robbie sitting in that group at a much younger age than I ever remember hearing ideas like these. It wasn't fair to ask her to do something like this right now and I would never presume to say that to her but the experience of her being there with Esther and my wife Jackie and all those good folks couldn't help but make it easier for her to do these things. It's like Galton said: "If I have seen great things in psychology it is because I have stood on the shoulders of great men."

Many people say to me, "Jess, how do you do those things that you do?" If there are any things that are exceptional that I do, it is because of the people who have loved me and because of the courage that has been given me by the people who have loved me and cared for me very deeply as some very special person.

To me this is the answer to the dilemma of what it is that I'm responsible for. Surrender to a higher-power— centered life is not something I can give to anyone else. It is only something I can work on for myself. As I let go more and more, it is easier to see that I am a perfect being. And the more I realize that, the more I avoid depressing and putting down the mind-body-spirit combination that you know as Jess. And the more I can literally transcend, the more I can literally redeem and restore the damage I have done in my body in those earlier times.

Because of living a different kind of life, I can tease out a maximum usefulness of the physical facilities, not just that I have but that are restored to me. And by living in harmony with what I am and what I have, there is a set of fantastic possibilities ahead for me. I don't need to look at them greedily and think, "My God, look at the wealth of living I'm going to pile up." I don't need to think about that. I don't know how much time is left to me but I know there is just enough time. I know there is plenty of time so that I don't need to hurry. I need to make each day count but I don't need to be frantic about making each day count.

It's like the man who sobered up at age sixty-four. A year later he wrote a beautiful article expressing his gratitude for his first year of sobriety. The title was "There Is a Life Before Death." He was grateful for what he was given instead of regretting all he had wasted.

I have all the time that's necessary. Were my plane to go down tomorrow, I will have all the time I need. There is no hurry. But I see that this ensures that I will make the very best use of my time. The person who is hurrying has to do the job four times. If they'd just slow up, they could do the job a little slower but do it just once. When we hurry, we miss everything.

There is just enough time. And this is why it is so absolutely necessary that I ally myself with people who see life this way and are working on life this way because then I don't need to throw away the society and move to Vilcabamba, Ecuador, where that community of long-lived people live. I can't speak their language, I can't live in their society. But there is a sub-society in this crazy Western civilization of ours that I can be a part of and that I can very carefully drift into and pull together and benefit from. That way I can spend my days in the company of people to whom I can occasionally say, without any self-consciousness at all, "Ain't I a wonder . . . and ain't you a wonder, too!" That helps quiet me down so I can see more clearly that, in my own small way, I love you.